In loving memory of my wonderful and godly parents,
Mr. and Mrs. Leroy and Lucy Brackins.
They taught me how to love, fear, reverence, and worship the Lord.
Their precious memories linger in my mind every day of my life.
They now sleep in the presence of the Lord,
awaiting our arrival in heaven.
In memory of my baby brother, Lionel, whose gifts from God were a
tremendous blessing to those who heard him sing.
Rest on.

Contents

SURRENDER to His Word

SERVICE in His Work

STEWARDSHIP *of* His Wealth

ACKNOWLEDGEMENTS

I am grateful to the Lord for blessing me with the desire and the spiritual strength to fulfill every assignment that He has placed before me.

I thank the Lord for the "Precious People" who comprise the membership of the Grace Tabernacle Missionary Bapticostal Church. It has been a joy and a delight beyond my ability to describe to be able to preach to you and teach you each week for more than twenty-five years.

I am grateful for my staff: Tara Jackson, Lafayette Kelly, Jerry Perry, John Hendrix, and John Bowie. All of you help me to be all that the Lord has called me to be in more ways than I can explain.

I thank the Lord for my extended family, my siblings, my children, my grandchildren, and my "Grace Gift, my Sweetie, my Prayer Partner, and my best Friend in the whole wide world," my wife, Pamela.

Thanks to all of you for praying for me, encouraging me, correcting me, and supporting me.

I love you all with my *WHOLE HEART.*

INTRODUCTION

As I look back, I thought it required all I had and all I knew just to begin and complete my first book, *A Marvelous Model of Ministry*, in 2008. Little did I know then that God was just getting ready to use me not only as a preacher of His Word and a pastor to His people, but also as an author. I praise Him for His overwhelming grace and for the privilege that He has afforded to me to be a source of inspiration to His precious people with this written presentation.

As I was preparing to embark upon this second project, it was clear from the Holy Spirit what subject matter He wanted me to share with His people. I have been led by the Lord to present this project in a three-fold format. Our time of sharing together is going to be focused on our *Surrender* to the *Word* of the *Lord,* our *Service* in the *Work* of the *Lord,* and our *Stewardship* with the *Wealth* of the *Lord.*

Preparing this material has been so exciting for me, and I hope and pray that what the Lord has allowed me to put in print will spiritually revolutionize your life to the glory of God. There are many Christians who no longer want to simply go through the motions of superficial religiosity, but now they are ready for a real relationship with the Lord. If this is you, then you have the right book in your hand. The Lord wants us to progress, mature, and flourish as we seek to enhance our relationship with Him and embrace our representation of Him. You were created by God to do more than simply occupy space and remain stuck on the treadmill of traditionalism.

As in my first publication, all of the material in this book is also based and founded on the principles from the Word of God. This is not a conglomeration of my own ideas, thoughts, opinions, or personal biases. Instead, each chapter contains a Biblical text, and each of the three sections are designed to provide a greater level of understanding, a greater level of inspiration, and a greater level of application of the Word of God in these specific areas.

Within these three areas, we need to demonstrate a greater level of our attention and commitment in order to be all that the Lord desires for us to be and to accomplish all that He desires for us to accomplish.

I believe that the Lord is going to transform your life and move you into a new level as it relates to your bond with Him by the time you have completed this book.

God bless you, and get ready to start "Making a Difference in the Kingdom of God."

The Cardinal, Brother Roy

Surrender
to the
Word of the Lord

CHAPTER 1

TOTALLY SURRENDERED TO JESUS CHRIST

Romans 6:16–18
SURRENDER

I am sure that those of us who are striving on a daily basis to become all that God desires for us to be would agree with my following statement. We are now living in a time when many people who call themselves Christians really have a casual approach to their relationships with the Lord. Then, to make matters even worse, many other people don't have a relationship with the Lord at all. Many people only pray when they are in a panic. They become annoyed when other people give God undignified praise, and they do not understand why some of us have no problem giving the Lord a tremendous amount of our time. Many people feel that God owes them the best that life has to offer while they give Him the least of what they have to offer in return. Many people have allowed the devil to cause them to settle for what Charles Stanley calls "casual Christianity."

We want the things of God to occur at a convenient time and require a convenient amount of effort. And God knows we only are willing to give a convenient amount of money to support the work of God. We have been misled—and diabolically deceived into believing—that what we need to do for ourselves, the money we need to spend on ourselves, and the time that we need to do our own thing is more important than what God is requiring and demanding from us. We have completely overlooked and obliterated from our minds the truth that Jesus Christ and His sacrifice at Calvary is the reason that we are still alive and not buried in our graves and on our way to hell.

One of the things that helps me put this matter of Christian responsibilities and my Godly obligations in their proper perspective is when I take the time to ask myself a very simple question: Where would I be if it had not been for the grace of God?

Despite all of the mistakes that we have made, promises that we have failed to keep, and times that we have gone contrary to the Word and the will of God, He just keeps on giving us chance after chance. And after all that God has done for us, we somehow feel as though we are offering God something special and that we are doing Him a favor when we decide to get up on Sunday, casually stroll into His house, and make our grand appearance. We think that when we come to church, we should not be challenged, our sins should not be mentioned, and our transgressions should not be called to our attention. We think that we should not be asked to give anything above and beyond our comfort zone, no matter how many people we may help with our gifts or regardless of the number of ministries that will have to suffer as a result of our failing to give our time, talent, and treasure. We don't want our feathers to be ruffled, we don't want to be made to feel uncomfortable, and we don't want to be told the consequences of not doing what God is commanding us to do in His Word. Many people only want a "feel-good religion": one that does not rub them the wrong way or cause them to look at their lifestyles and examine why they keep making the same ungodly and destructive choices and decisions over and over again.

I want to begin our time together by getting right to where the rubber meets the road. Jesus is not interested in having a part-time relationship with us. He is not going to allow us to treat Him as some Godly sugar daddy who just takes care *of* us without also requiring something *from* us. Christianity is a *relationship*. And a relationship is not a one-way street; it is a two-way street. He has saved us, so now we must serve Him. He has died for us, so now we must be devoted to Him. He has redeemed us, so now we must represent Him. He has filled us, so now we must be faithful to Him. He has provided for us, so now we must produce for

Him. He has lifted us, so now we must live for Him. He has cleansed us, so now we must be committed to Him. He has transformed us, so now we must testify about Him. And He has guarded, guided, and governed us, so now the very least we can do is bring glory to Him.

I need to ask you several questions: What more do you want God to do for you before you will become willing to do more for Him? How many more prayers do you want Him to answer? How many more bills do you want Him to pay? How many more doors do you want Him to open? How many more enemies do you want Him to make leave you alone? How many more nights do you want Him to rock you to sleep? How many more mornings do you want Him to wake you up? How many more meals do you want Him to put on your table? And how many more of your sins do you want Him to forgive? How many more times do you want Him to heal your body?

I want us all to realize that we should never reach a position of complacency in our relationship with the Lord. We should be always striving to reach new platitudes of spiritual excellence in our walk with Jesus Christ. The very fact that we are still alive and able to address this matter of becoming more committed to the Lord helps us to recognize how much we take our relationship with Him for granted. And if you don't believe me, just let me prove my point. How many times do you attend classes each week and receive instruction on the importance of working to provide for yourself? How many times do you attend classes each week and receive instruction on the need to shop for yourself? How many times do you attend classes each week to receive instruction on the importance of getting your hair done, your clothes cleaned, taking vacations, or discovering the importance of going to the movies? The answer is *none*, because all of these things are important to us—but they are all temporary. Yet we have to be reminded week after week of the importance of paying the tithe, coming to Bible study, becoming active in a ministry, sharing our faith, walking in holiness, praying, forgiving, praising, and remaining committed and consistent in our relationship with the Lord—and all of these are eternal things.

In Romans Chapter 6, Paul is trying to get us to understand that we all will be a servant to somebody or something. We will either serve the Lord Jesus Christ and be His slave or we will serve the devil and be his slave. We simply have to ask ourselves whom we feel can take better care of us: the Lord or the devil.

In addition, in Romans Chapter 6, Paul refers to us as slaves. This means that we do not own ourselves, but we have been bought with a price. We now belong to God. Notice the language Paul uses in verse 16. He asks a rhetorical question: "Do you not know that to whom you present yourselves slaves to obey, you are that one's slaves whom you obey, whether of sin leading to death, or of obedience leading to righteousness?" This helps us understand the importance of evaluating how and why we make:

I: The Decision

In Paul's letter to the Romans, he wants us to understand that God will not and is not going to force Himself on us. The Lord will reveal His purpose to us, He will express His love for us, and He will even display His ability to provide for us. But it is up to us to accept what He is offering by yielding to Him completely. Did you not know that whatever we yield to is what we become slave to? The crack addict has yielded to the crack pipe, and he will do whatever is necessary to get his next hit. The alcoholic has yielded to the bottle, and he will do whatever is necessary to get his next drink. Gluttons have yielded to food, and they will do whatever is necessary to satisfy their cravings and appetites. The gambler has yielded to the dice table, the craps table, or the blackjack table or to placing bets on sporting events and will do whatever is necessary to place the next wager. All these things lead to nothing but heartache and shame.

To place this in its proper perspective, I asked the following questions of our congregation one Sunday in worship: Is there anybody in the house who has become a slave to worship and just can't get enough of church? Is there anybody in the house who has become a slave to Bible study and just can't get here soon enough? Is there anybody here who has become a slave to prayer and just can't wait for another opportunity to call on the Lord in supplication? Is there anybody here who has become a slave to reading the Word of God and the first thing you do every morning is spend some time with God and the Bible?

> We all should have a desire to be even better saints for the Lord than we were sinners for the devil, and all of us were some real good sinners.

As a matter of fact, a few of us are still pretty good at that old, sinful lifestyle. We must reach a point where we make up our minds and make a consistent and a committed decision to yield totally to Jesus Christ without holding anything back from Him. Too many of us have allowed the devil to deceive us into believing that complete surrender to the Lord will cause us to miss out on some of the good things in life. But the exact opposite is true. When we completely surrender to Him, we discover all the joy, peace, blessings, favor, grace, mercy, provisions, and inheritance that He already has in store and laid out for us.

I have discovered that one of the reasons so many of us are hesitant to surrender completely to our Lord is because we have a poor and distorted image of who He really is. And the reason we have the wrong image of Him is because we have allowed everybody to tell us what God is like except for His Son as He presents Him in His Holy Word, the Bible. Paul says when we become slaves to sin and obey the devil, we will find ourselves being totally separated from God because that kind of lifestyle leads to death. But when we obey the Lord and His Word, it will lead to righteousness, and God always blesses righteousness. The decision is up to you, but you will serve somebody. Whatever choice you make, you will have to live with it throughout eternity.

Then in Romans Chapter 6, verse 17, we read, "But God be thanked that though you were slaves of sin, yet you obeyed from the heart that form of doctrine to which you were delivered." This helped me understand that if we are going to be totally committed and surrendered to Jesus Christ, we need to make the right decision. But we also need to recognize that He is the only One who can provide our:

II: Deliverance

Notice how Paul begins verse 17 writing about God's deliverance. He says, "But God be thanked...." Reading this motivated me to stop for a moment and thank God for delivering me and setting me free from the shackles of sin. Can you look back over your life and thank God for the fact that you are no longer held hostage by the enemy and are no longer a prisoner of satan? You are no longer a captive to sin, and you are no longer bound for hell. But now our souls have been saved. Our names have been changed, our sins have been forgiven, our futures have been secured, our faith has been established, our joy has been restored, our purpose has been discovered, our robes have been washed, our feet have been planted, and our hearts have been cleansed. Do you know that if it had not been for the Lord being on your side, you would have been cut off a long time ago? Paul says we should be able to thank God for the fact that we used to be slaves to sin, but now we are sons of righteousness.

I want to emphasize that Jesus is the Son of God, and He became the slave of God. When He died for us, Jesus was fulfilling a dualistic responsibility. As a Son, He was being obedient to His Father and fulfilling His assignment. But as a slave, He was being explicitly obedient to His Father by dying for sins that He did not even commit. Many of us want to enjoy the blessings of being God's sons, but we don't want to fulfill the responsibilities and requirements of being God's slaves. We should be proud to let the world know that Jesus is our Master and that we yield and surrender to His authority and His plans every day of our lives.

Paul also tells us how the change has been made in our lives. It is not because we decided to get our lives together or because we enrolled in some self-improvement classes. We have been set free and delivered from sin because we obeyed from our hearts the doctrine from the Word of God. And misunderstanding the reason for change is where the problem lies with many people. They join the church because they are feeling emotional, guilty, or sorry for themselves. But when you become attached to the church, it should be because you have heard the truth from the Word of God. The same Word that caught you will also keep you. Whenever people join our church and do not complete new member orientation, come to Bible Study, come to Sunday School, or become attached to a specific ministry, we quickly figure out that the Word of God is not too important to them. We do not expect such unengaged members to have a lasting impact on the lives of other people in a positive way.

Then finally, in verse 18, Paul says, "And having been set free from sin, you became slaves of righteousness." Paul helps us understand that if we are going to become totally committed and surrendered to Jesus Christ, we must start by making the right decision. We must learn how to praise God for His deliverance. And the final piece to the puzzle is our:

III: Daily Dedication

What this verse is trying to teach us is that we have an advantage over those people who suffered as slaves before it was abolished under the Declaration of Independence. Those people could not choose their slave masters. Paul says we chose the devil out of ignorance, and now we have the option of making a better choice. That choice is Jesus. If you have not made that choice, allow me to suggest at least three reasons why you should choose Jesus. 1) He is the One who *created* you in His own image. 2) He is the One who *redeemed you from the hand of the devil*. 3) He is the One who is waiting to *fill you with His Holy Spirit*. And that should be enough for you to have a desire to become totally surrendered to Jesus Christ!

CHAPTER 2

MOVING BEYOND THE MASQUERADE

Romans 12:2
SURRENDER

I believe one of the greatest hindrances to our ability to lead other people to Jesus Christ is not found simply in our inability to talk about Jesus. It's in our failure to consistently live the kind of lives that really epitomize what real Christianity is all about. When I was a little boy, older people would call this kind of behavior talking out of both sides of your mouth, meaning that people were guilty of saying pious things but living the kind of life that did not coincide with the words that they spoke. Someone has written, "I can't hear what you are saying because what you are doing is speaking too loudly." Whether we admit it or not, people don't listen to what we say for very long. Our actions leave a lasting impression on people—either positively or negatively.

Many of us are quick in our attempts to justify our worldly and ungodly activities by saying, "Well, you know, Jesus also mingled with sinners." This is absolutely correct. While He did spend time with sinners, Jesus always made them feel uncomfortable in their sins, and He never mingled with them to win their approval. Instead, He mingled with them in an attempt to save their souls from a burning hell. I do not believe that Jesus is opposed to us mingling with sinners. He just wants us to change them and not be changed by them. We are the salt of the earth and the light of the world, and the goal should be to set the standard and not blend in with the crowd. The goal should be to raise the bar and not let our guards down. Our goals should be centered on leading people into a saving relationship with Jesus Christ and not gaining them as our personal cheering squads.

I have discovered that many people who are in the world and out of the church remain in their uncommitted condition for too long of a time. These people stay away from church because they see many Christians who are supposedly connected to Jesus Christ doing the same things, going the same places, talking the same way, and behaving in the same manner as they do. And to them, our relationship with Christ does not seem to be genuine and sincere but simply a once-a-week, Sunday-only masquerade. We need to be reminded that the Lord is still looking for some sold-out, connected, committed, consecrated, and consistent Christians, who will live *for* Him and live *like* Him all day and every day of our lives. As believers in Jesus Christ, we must acknowledge that there are some things Christians should not do, say, and go, unless we are going there with the exclusive intent to lead someone out of their repulsive demonic darkness and into the refulgent, luminous light of Jesus Christ. Many who claim to be a part of the body of Christ really want to be able to party with the devil all week and then shout with the saints on Sunday.

But have you taken a moment to consider that we really don't need many Christians in the church-house? The church-house represents our comfort and safety zone. We really need more Christians who will represent Jesus in the workplace, at the ball game, at the shopping mall, at the movie theater, at the barbershop, at the beauty salon, and in our schools. The Lord is not interested in pretentious people who are only able to put up a good front in His house without having any real significant substance in their daily walk with Christ. If we are going to be able to fulfill the Great Commission of Jesus Christ, which instructs us to go into all the world and preach the gospel and make disciples of all people, then we need to realize that we must exhibit that there has been a change in our lives before we can convince the world that they need a change in their lives. It is impossible for me to try to convince an alcoholic to surrender his life to Christ if we are sitting at the same bar trying to drown our sorrows away together. It is impossible for me to try to convince a shake dancer to forsake her shake-dancing ways if the two of us are regular patrons of the same shake-dancing club.

In Romans Chapter 12, Paul helps us tremendously with the internal ingredients for effective soul-winning before we even attempt to exercise the external responsibilities. Verse 2 of this chapter reads, "And do not be conformed to this world, but be transformed by the renewing of your mind, that you may prove what is that good and acceptable and perfect will of God." The New Living Translation renders verse 2 as, "Don't copy the behavior and the customs of this world, but let God transform you into a new person by changing the way you think. Then you will know what God wants you to do, and you will know how good and pleasing and perfect His will really is."

I believe Paul wants us to understand that it's time for us to take off our masks, come out of our costumes, remove the superficial facades from our demeanors, and become the people both inside and out—day in and day out—that God would have us be. In the first verse of this chapter, Paul uses the word "beseech" as it relates to his desire for us to present our bodies as a living sacrifice unto God. He calls this our reasonable service. This word "beseech" is really an intense prayer. It is his way of pleading with us to present ourselves to God as a living sacrifice. If we offer ourselves completely to God, there is nothing left of us to be used by the world or the devil. But many of us only offer a little bit of ourselves to God, and we wind up leaving a whole lot for the devil to work with. After Paul pleads with us in verse 1 to offer ourselves totally to God, he then explains how we can be used most effectively by God: "And do not be conformed to this world." If we are going to move beyond the masquerade, we must:

I: Resist the Temptations

When he uses the term "this world," Paul means we are *in* the world but not *of* the world. When I am striving to help people to understand this principle, I explain:

> To be in the world and not of the world is like a boat designed to sail on top of the water. If too much water gets into the boat, the boat will soon be sunk by what it was intended to rise above.

Whenever we allow too much of the world to get into our lives, we will find ourselves sinking into the sinful muck and mire of this world as opposed to rising above the evil that is everywhere in this world in which we live. God will not hide sinful temptations from us, but He will give us the power and the authority to say no to the devil and not allow temptation to defeat or overtake us. God did not hide the tree of life and the tree of good and evil from Adam and Eve in the Garden of Eden. But He did specifically tell them not to eat from the tree. Notice Paul's language. He writes, "And do not be conformed to this world." This word "conformed" means to fashion yourself according to what you see in the world. We may not want to have it called to our attention, we may not want to hear about it, and we may not even want to deal with it, but the truth is, we are so easily swayed by what we see in the world and are quick to fashion our lives like the lives of those in the world. We quickly adjust to the trends of our society without even taking the time to ask ourselves:

Does this image I am portraying reveal more of the world in me than it does of the God in me?

How do we deal with the temptation to surrender to the ways of the world? We must keep the cross of Calvary between the world and us. When we always look to the cross, it reminds us that we are supposed to be a reflection of Christ who suffered, died, and was resurrected for us and not a reflection of the devil who wanted to condemn us to the pit of hell. Many Christian believers fail to take the time to ask themselves why we would even want to look and act like the devil, considering all the negative things he has done and still desires to do to us. Do you not realize that the devil held us as prisoners to sin before Jesus set us free? The devil separated us from God; he caused us to suffer pain, and many of us still have the scars. Because of the devil, we have done things that have broken God's heart, we have said things that caused His kingdom to suffer shame, and we have gone places that crippled our witness. Why would we want to look like the world? The world has caused us to shed tears and face doubt, rejection, and humiliation. Why would we want to conform to the world when the world desires to suck the life out of us and then throw us away like yesterday's garbage? Why would we want to look like the devil and conform to the image of this world when the world's greatest desire is to cause us to spend eternity in a burning hell and separate us forever from God? If we are going to be able to move beyond the masquerade, we must learn how to resist the temptation to conform to this world.

In this same verse, we read these following words: "But be ye transformed by the renewing of your mind." This helps us to understand that if we are going to move beyond the masquerade, we must not only resist the temptation, but we must also:

II: Reveal our Transformation before the world.

Before I move into the intricate details of this part of the verse, allow me to ask one very important question. What good did it do for God to have allowed His Son Jesus to die to save you from your sins if nobody knows about it but you and the Lord?

The second half of this verse helps us understand that some things God tells us *not to do* and other things that God tells us *to do*. He tells us *not to be* conformed to this world, and then He tells us *to be* transformed by the renewing of our minds. This word "transformed" is really our English word, "metamorphosis." The change that shows up on the outside actually takes place because of a new nature on the inside.

Most of us are familiar with butterflies. We love to watch them fly in all of their beauty. But we need to remember that butterflies started off as caterpillars. Caterpillars are not delicate and lovely like butterflies, and they can seem destructive, but after the metamorphosis has taken place inside a cocoon, they are beautiful and desirable when they emerge outside in the world. Jesus Christ has done this for us: we were destructive caterpillar creatures of sin, but at Calvary, He transformed us into beautiful butterflies of God's amazing grace. Why would we even consider returning to our caterpillar condition when God has transformed us into His blessed, beautiful butterflies? The only way a caterpillar can become a butterfly is for there to be a change on the inside. The only way we can reveal our transformation is to renew our minds.

The first part of this verse deals with the need to *control our desires*, and the second part of this verse deals with the need to *concentrate on our development*. This word "renewing" means renovating your mind. There must be a consistent pattern of taking the old, worldly stuff out of our minds and adding more godly thoughts, plans, goals, and truths to our minds. Our minds will not be renewed automatically; we must put forth the effort. This is why Paul tells us to "be transformed by the renewing of your mind."

The devil wants to keep your mind on old habits, ways, sins, relationships, activities, and hangouts. The devil will do everything he possibly can to keep you from having a renewed mind, because he knows that when your mind is renewed, your life will become a shining example for Jesus Christ. When your mind is renewed, your praise will elevate to another level. When your mind is renewed, your giving will increase. When your mind is renewed, your witness will become effective. When your mind is renewed, your prayer life will expand. When your mind is renewed, your patience will develop. When your mind is renewed, your participation in church will become consistent. When your mind is renewed, your family will become stronger. When your mind is renewed, your life will become productive. When your mind is renewed, you will come to realize that greater is He who is in you than he who is in the world.

When we have a renewed mind on the inside, there should be a noticeable change on the outside. That is precisely why I believe Paul concludes verse 2 with "that you may prove what is that good and acceptable and perfect will of God." When we learn how to *resist the temptations* to become conformed to the standards of the world, and then we learn the importance of *revealing our transformation* to the world, we are then ready to:

III: Release our Testimony to the World

Paul writes, "That you may **prove** what is *good, acceptable* and the *perfect* will of God." God has high standards and expectations for all of His children. This word "prove" is *doekeemodzo* in the Greek language, and it means to put to the test, scrutinize, and see if something is genuine after a careful examination. God wants us to have diamond divinity and to get rid of our counterfeit cubic zirconium Christianity. Paul is saying that the Lord wants to put our works to the test, not just on Sunday morning but also when we are in stressful situations or when we are tempted to just go along with the crowd. The Lord is looking for people that He can use to release a genuine testimony before the world. This verse lets us know that He wants our works to pass three major test categories. He wants them to be good, acceptable, and usable to display the perfect will of God.

This word "good" means to be useful and filled with joy. The Lord is looking for people who are willing to be used by Him and serve Him not with a spirit of obligation, but with a disposition of joyful excitement. Do you have anything *good* to offer the Lord? Is there any joy in your service?

Then Paul goes on to write the word "acceptable," which means well pleasing. In other words, when we offer the Lord our service, we should have just one thing on our minds: to make sure that He is pleased. Don't worry about people criticizing you as long as you know the Lord will say, "Well done, my good and faithful servant."

Finally, Paul uses the term, "the perfect will of God." At first these words were difficult for me to read, because the Bible teaches us that no one is perfect but God. So I wanted to know how we could possibly display the "perfect will of God." I discovered that "perfect" does not mean being flawless. It means being mature and complete. We must learn how to give the Lord all that we have and leave absolutely nothing behind. And when we have made up our minds to give God all that we have, we are then ready to move beyond the masquerade. Playtime is over, and we are now ready for serious business. It's time for us to pursue God's will for our lives. God knows what He wants to do with and through us, and it is all based on what He has already done for us.

Allow me to help you imagine a Sunday morning worship experience at Grace Tabernacle and remind you of what God has done for us. He did not give us a second-class salvation, and we should not offer Him second-class service! He gave us His perfect Son, so the least we can do is offer Him our good, acceptable, and perfect service. Let me tell you just a little about God's perfect gift to us. His name is Jesus. He came for us. He walked among us. He healed us, fed us, and clothed us, and one

Friday He died for us. Early one Sunday morning, He rose from the grave for our salvation. Since He was willing to do all of this for us, the least we can do is offer Him our very best service!

Remove that mask, surrender to the Lord, and offer Him your best, because He deserves nothing less.

CHAPTER 3

THE KIND OF FAITH THAT PLEASES THE LORD

Hebrews 11:7
SURRENDER

I have known so many people who have been going through seasons of difficulty in their lives, and they have made the following statement more times than I can count: "I only wish I had more faith." To clarify, if you have been born again and if you truly have an eternal relationship with Jesus Christ, you do not need more faith. All you need to do is learn how to use and exercise the faith that you already have. The Bible tells us that faith comes by hearing the Word of God. In Luke 17:5, the apostles came to Jesus and said, "Lord, increase our faith." Jesus then responded to them by saying, "If you have faith as a mustard seed, you can say to this mulberry tree, 'Be pulled up by the roots and be planted into the sea,' and it will obey you." I believe the Lord wanted to teach us that it is not the size of our faith that will change our circumstances; it is the effectiveness of our faith that will turn our situations around. God is not looking for us to have a greater amount of faith, just a greater activation of the faith that He has already given to us.

I have discovered that many of us are willing to use our faith—our trust and belief that the person will keep a promise to us—in every area of our lives except in our relationship with Jesus Christ. As an illustration, when we pay our electricity bills on time, we are not surprised when we come home and our lights are still on. When we pay our cell phone bills, we are not surprised when we turn our phone on and can still make calls and receive calls. When we make our car loan payments on time, we are not surprised when our cars have not been repossessed. We have faith in these worldly institutions. Yet we become frantic, hesitant, and disobedient when it is time for us to honor the Lord with our money, time, and talents, because the devil has tricked us into believing that God will not honor His word, so we take matters into our own hands.

In the preceding verse of this same chapter of the book of Hebrews, we are told, "But without faith, it is impossible to please God, for He is a rewarder of those who diligently seek Him." God is a *rewarder* for those who diligently seek Him. "Rewarder" means that God honors and keeps His Word. "Diligently" means to seek Him with a passion and to never give up until you have come into His presence. The writer of this book wants us to ask ourselves, what is the use of worshipping God if we don't believe that God is going to honor His word? And if we *do believe* that He will honor His word, why do we ever doubt Him, distrust Him, and disobey Him when things get dark and dismal in our lives? Do you serve a God who cannot be trusted when the chips are down in your life? The only way that our faith is going to be developed is by trusting the Lord against all odds and by learning that He is not a man that He should lie. His promise is that "heaven and earth will pass away before one jot or tittle" of His Word shall fail.

This is a lesson that a prominent human character in the Bible learned in his relationship with the Lord. Noah had many imperfections, just like many of us. He lived during a time when wickedness on the earth was abounding everywhere, just like us. People laughed at him because of his relationship with the Lord, just like us. But unlike many of us is, Noah was willing to obey the Lord even when he did not completely understand what God was about to do with him and through him.

Now, to really understand all that Noah was challenged by God to accomplish, we refer to Chapter 6 of Genesis. We are told that there was great wickedness on the earth and that the hearts and thoughts of all people were only toward evil. They went to bed with sin on their minds, they woke up in the morning with sin on their minds, and they spent every waking moment only thinking about how they could sin more today than they had sinned yesterday. The Bible tells us that God was sorry that He had made humanity and was grieved in His heart. The Lord was about to destroy all of His creation. We read in verse 8 of Genesis Chapter 6 that "Noah found grace in the eyes of the Lord." In other words, in the midst of all of this evil debauchery, gross immorality, escalating antipathy, permeating profligacy, depraved decadence, and licentious lifestyles, the Lord found one man named Noah who was striving to walk like Him and live a holy life.

The Lord told Noah to build an ark because He was about to destroy the earth with the waters of a flood. We must understand that it had never rained on the earth before, so Noah did not even know what a flood was. But despite his lack of understanding, he still obeyed the Lord. True faith and total surrender really are obeying what God tells us to do, even when we don't understand why the Lord is telling us to do it.

Hebrews chapter 11, verse 7, says, "By faith, Noah, being divinely warned of things not yet seen, moved with fear..."

I: Noah Believed God

Notice the first two words of the verse: "by faith." Noah did not move by sight, he did not move by impulse, he did not move according to good advice, he did not move because of sound logical reasoning, and he did not move because of outside humanistic pressure. But Noah moved by faith and by faith alone. Do you have enough faith to believe God even when you cannot understand God? There are a whole lot of things that I cannot understand, but my lack of understanding does not stop me from believing in them or trusting in them. I don't understand how a machine called an airplane—that weighs more than six tons, carries more than two hundred passengers, and flies at thirty-five thousand feet in the air and at the speed of five hundred miles per hour—can do what it does. But when they tell me to board the plane, I obey. When they tell me to buckle my seat belt, I obey. When they tell me to store my carry-on luggage and place my tray table in an upright and locked position, I obey. I have found out that if I want to get to my destination, I must obey the people who are in charge of flying this massive machine.

We need to ask ourselves if it is possible that many of us have not reached our destination because we are too stubborn to believe in the Lord, surrender to the Lord, and obey the Lord simply because we cannot understand what He is up to. Noah was a man who allowed His beliefs to move him to a position of activity. In other words, if we believe God, we should obey God. If God says pay the tithe, just do it and give Him a chance to keep His word. If the Lord says forgive, release that bitterness and those grudges and watch Him make your enemies your footstools. If the Lord says, "Let everything that has breath praise the Lord," just praise Him and watch Him show up right in the midst of your praise.

Noah was a man of faith not only because he believed God. Verse 7 goes on to say, "He prepared an ark for the saving of his household." That lets me know that:

II: Noah Built for God

The Lord told Noah to build an ark because it was going to flood on the earth, and it had never even rained before. Now, I could not really appreciate this until I compared it to some of the things that the Lord has challenged me to do in my ministry. For example, the Lord told me to lead Grace Tabernacle in several building projects, and I did not know where the money was coming from. But I cannot even imagine the Lord telling me to build a church, and nobody before me had ever built one. Our faith today should be stronger than that of the people in the Bible, because in many instances, they were the first ones to experience what they went through. But now, at least we can reference what the Lord did in their lives. When we got ready to build Grace Tabernacle, I had some examples that I could use to help strengthen my faith. I could think of Pastor Albert Chew and how the Lord used him to build the Shiloh Baptist Church. Or, I could think of Pastor B. R. Daniels Sr. and how the Lord used him in building the Beth Eden Baptist Church. Or I could think of my own pastor, William Bowie Jr., and how the Lord used him in building the True Light Baptist Church.

But Noah had nobody to compare his building project to. Noah could not look to Moses for advice; he had not been born yet. He could not look to David or Solomon for architectural tips, because they were not even on the scene yet. What Noah did was a true act of faith.

Noah's building of this ark reveals at least three things that all of us should possess when we are striving to do something extraordinary for the Lord. First, he was *committed.* He kept working for 120 years in the midst of a deluge of criticism and scorn from the people who were around him, and he did not have one drop of rain as evidence that his work was not in vain. Second, he was *courageous.* He did not allow the distracters and the naysayers to dissuade or discourage him. Third, he was *creative.* He did not build a canoe.

> **He did not build a fishing boat; he did not build a float. He built an ark, and he used the best materials that he could find, because he knew that other people were going to have to ride in what he was building.**

The Bible says, "Noah prepared an ark for the saving of his household." This helped me understand that the only way that I can save my household is when I learn to walk by faith and obey God, even when it does not seem to make sense.

How safe would other people feel about riding in what you are building for the Lord with your time, talent, and treasure? Are there any leaks in your building because you are using cheap building materials? What the ark was to the Old Testament, the cross is to the New Testament. When Jesus died at Calvary, He died on a cross that was able to hold the sins of the whole world. *He did not die on a limb; He did not die on a branch.* He died on something that could hold Him and everybody else who wanted to become a part of His kingdom. And if you really want something to shout about, here it is. Noah not only used his own physical strength to build this ark, but he also used his own financial resources to build something that did not even make sense. Do the commands of the Lord have to make sense to you before you will invest your financial resources in His work?

Noah *believed* the Lord. Noah *built* for the Lord. But the text goes on to say, "by which he condemned the world." This lets me know also:

III: Noah Behaved Like the Lord

When the Bible says, "he condemned the world," this simply means that Noah's godly moral character caused the ungodly people to see how wicked they were, and he did not have to say one word. He just walked in the ways of God. He lived as a child of God should live. When everybody else was saying yes to sin and wickedness, Noah was saying no to the devil's temptations. When everybody else was blending in and going along with the crowd, Noah was breaking away from the crowd. His faith condemned their faithlessness. Some people will get upset with you when you are a tither or a grace-giver, are involved in several ministries, and are praying for people every week while they do nothing but take God's grace for granted. Your faith will condemn them, just as Noah's faith condemned the people in his generation.

Finally, the verse ends by saying that Noah "became heir of the righteousness which is according to faith." Noah *believed* God, Noah built for God, and Noah behaved like God. In closing:

IV: Noah Was Blessed By God

The Bible says that he "became heir of the righteousness which is according to faith." If we plan to inherit anything from God, we must have faith in Him and be willing to surrender to Him. Vance Havner says faith is an acronym for:

Forsaking All I Trust Him.

We cannot trust the Lord and hold on to our own plans at the same time. But when we let go, the Lord will show up in a mighty way in our lives. There were animals on that ark, but the Bible does not describe any restroom facilities. There was mess on that ark, just like there is mess in the church. But those who stayed on the inside with the mess were saved while those on the outside were lost. I did not get to ride on the first ark that Noah built. But have become attached to the cross that Jesus carried. I was not there when He sacrificed His life, but by faith, I believe that He did die. He was buried, and early Sunday morning, He got us with all power. Since He loved me enough to die for me, I have surrendered so that I might serve Him.

CHAPTER 4

The Bigger the Risk, The Bigger the Reward

Hebrews 11:8
Surrender

In my humble opinion, the most profound statement that I will make in this chapter will not be made during one of my points of emphasis or toward the end of the chapter, but it will be made right here at the beginning. The statement is that the Lord appears to us suddenly and unannounced and challenges our faith at times when we would least expect Him to manifest His presence in our lives. For example, the Lord showed up to Moses on the back side of the desert while he was minding his own business and tending to his father-in-law's sheep. He showed up to David, a shepherd boy, while he was working in the backyard of his father's house. He showed up to Elijah while he was having a pity party under a juniper tree. He showed up to a young virgin named Mary while she was perhaps playing with her dolls and just learning how to wear lipstick. He showed up to James and John while they were cleaning their fishing nets with their father, Zebedee. He showed up to Matthew while he was at his place of employment, the tax-collecting office. He showed up to Paul while he was on his way to persecute Christians on the Damascus road. And He showed up in my life right after I had finished playing in a rock and roll concert in December of 1973 and literally turned my life right side up, because it was already upside down.

I have discovered that many of us think that the Lord owes us some advance warning. Or we think He should at least send us a two-week notice to inform us that He is about to challenge our faith and move us out of our comfort zone, whether we are ready for it or not. Nowhere is this truer than in the life of a principle humanistic character in the Bible, Abraham. To really understand how the Lord, in the words of our younger generation, "rolled up on Abraham," we need to take the time to read Genesis Chapter 12, where we will make an amazing discovery.

In verse 1 of Genesis Chapter 12, we read, "Now the Lord had said to Abram: Get out of your country, from your family, and from your father's house, to a land that I will show you. I will make you a great nation; I will bless you and make your name great; and you shall be a blessing. I will bless those who bless you, and I will curse him who curses you; and in you all the families of the earth shall be blessed."

Now if this was not a statement of shock, I don't know what is. The Lord comes to Abram, as he was known before the Lord changed his name to Abraham, and tells him to leave family, friends, and his familiar surroundings. And all he had to go on was a promise from God. This man was minding his own business, trying to do his own thing, and doing his best to take care of his family, and the Lord tells him, "I am about to do something extraordinary in your life, and all I need you to do is to surrender to me, trust me and take me at my Word." Now before you are too shocked, allow me to also share this priceless and precious principle with you. Whenever the Lord gives us a great faith challenge that requires total surrender, He also gives us a great promise attached to the challenge. The Lord tells Abraham to leave family, friends, and familiar surroundings, but He also tells him that He is going to make him a great nation, bless those who bless him, and curse those who curse him. In other words, the bigger the risk for God, the bigger the rewards from God! All Abraham had to go on was the Word of God and the promises of God. Here I will ask the question:

> **If you cannot trust in God's promises, what does He need to do to gain your confidence?**

The Lord appeared to Abraham unannounced and unexpected and gave him the greatest faith challenge that he had ever experienced in his life. And this just may be the point where you are in your relationship with the Lord. The Lord has allowed you to be reading this chapter at this very pivotal point in your life, and He wants to challenge you to get off the sidelines, move out of your comfort zone, lay down your do-nothing attitude, and become active in His kingdom. And He did not even give you any advance notice before you decided to buy this book. The Lord has allowed you to have the ability to read so He could get in your face and ask you some hard questions and present you with some hard faith challenges. The Lord is about to give us the example of Abraham, who took Him at His word, and He never let him down. And He told me to tell you that He is able to do the very same thing in your life if you will just trust Him, surrender to Him, and walk with Him by faith!

Notice how this part of the story begins in verse 8: "By faith Abraham obeyed when he was called to go out..." It is there that we see:

I: His Surrender to the Purpose of God

Now allow me to tell you something that absolutely blew my mind. When Abraham obeyed the Lord, all he had was the Word of God and the promise of God. He was not like many of us; he did not have the benefit of having the King James Version of the Bible. He did not have the New King James Version or the NIV translation. He did not have the New American Standard Bible, the Living Bible, or the Messenger Bible. He did not have CDs to play while he drove in his car. He did not have Bible-study notes that he could use as inspiration. He did not have the option of enrolling in seminary or attending a conference for developing his faith. He did not have the option of meeting with his pastor to seek advice as to whether he should listen to the Lord or make another decision. He did not have the pleasure of attending a revival or a worship service where the preacher would have a book available for his reading entitled, *Making a Difference in the Kingdom of God* (I just could not resist that).

And to make matters even more complicated, his own father, Terah, was not a true worshipper and follower of Jehovah. As a matter of fact, some historical documents tell us that he was a chief idol worshipper. But in the midst of all this, Abraham was still willing to trust and believe in the Word of God and the promises of God. And I can't help but wonder why our faith is so weak and our trust so feeble. We have so many more advantages, and the challenges before us are not nearly as great. Notice again what the verse shares with us. "By faith Abraham obeyed when he was called." He did not have to be forced to obey, he did not have to be convinced to obey, and God did not have to punish him to get him to obey. All he did was hear and obey the voice of God.

Now some of you may be wondering if the Lord trying to get you to move and leave your family, friends, and familiar surroundings so you can prove my faith to Him. The answer is *yes*! I imagine that was not the answer that you were expecting, so allow me to elaborate. Not all moves are physical, geographical moves. Some of us need to move *mentally*. We need to learn how to think more like the Lord. We have people around us who are hindering us daily from being all that the Lord desires us to be. We will never grow until we either move them or move ourselves. Then some of us need to move in our *ministry*. We are stuck at the same level where we have been for the past six years. I have shared with people all across this country the following principle.

Wherever you are in ministry, you are in a "no-parking zone." Cars that are parked in a no-parking zone are susceptible to being towed away. And whenever you are towed, it always costs you more to get your vehicle back than you were intending to spend.

Some of us need to move *mentally*, some need to move in our *ministry*, and some need to move *monetarily* in their relationship with the Lord. Whenever you are walking with the Lord by faith, you have to be prepared to invest whatever you have into His hands. The Lord told Abraham to leave all the stuff back at his father's house and his family. The next part of the verse explains how Abraham was able to trust the Lord the way that he did: "He was called out to the place which he would receive as an inheritance." Abraham not only had faith to surrender to the purpose of God, but he also had enough faith to help him

II: Secure the Possessions of God

Allow me to share something with you that blessed me tremendously. The Lord will never allow us to give up something good for Him without Him replacing it with something better! Abraham was leaving a land where he was serving other people, and God was getting ready to take him to a land where other people would be serving him. In Genesis 12:2–3, God said, "I will make you a great nation…I will bless those who bless you and I will curse him who curses you…" At this point in his life, Abraham did not even have his own family, because he and Sarah had no children. But the Lord told him, "I am not only going to make you into a great family, I am going to make you into a great nation." Abraham never would have been known as the "father of the faithful," if he had been content with what he already had and not taken the Lord at his word.

Many of us will never receive all that the Lord has for us, because our lack of faith will not allow us to trust God beyond what we can figure out in our own minds. Trusting God will never make sense, but it does lead to some tremendous blessings. And if you are waiting on your budget to balance out before you start tithing, you will never see the windows of heaven open up to you. If you are waiting for your personal skills to improve before you join a ministry, you will never see God work a miracle through you. If you are waiting for your work schedule to change before you become more committed, you will never see God do the impossible in your life. Logic says, "I must see it, then I will believe it." But faith and surrender say, "God said it, and I believe it, even though I cannot see it right now."

The Bible tells us that Abraham "was called by God to go to a place that he would receive as an inheritance." Where he was living when the Lord called him, he had to work for it. But the Lord was leading him to a place where he would receive his inheritance. And when I looked up this word "inheritance," here is what I found out. An inheritance is something that is passed down from one person to another person without the receiving person having to do any work to gain it. Are you ready to shout again? Well here it is! The inheritance was not coming from his father or any of his family. The inheritance was not coming from any familiar sources, but the Lord was about to take land that was in Abraham's enemy's hands and place it in Abraham's hands. And it was not going to cost him one dime! When we learn how to walk with the Lord by faith, he is able to take property out of our enemies' hands and place it in our hands. The bigger the risk, the bigger the reward. But we will never receive all that the Lord has for us until we become mentally prepared for Him to confront us when we least expect it with a challenge to our faith unlike anything we have ever experienced before.

Abraham surrendered to the purpose of God, and he secured the possessions of God, but the verse ends by saying, "And he went out not knowing where he was going." This helped me to understand that he was also:

III: Surrounded by the Protection of God

Abraham started traveling, and the Lord did not even give him a compass, a map, or an atlas. But Abraham did have a GPS system: not a Global Positioning System, but a Godly Protection System. And that was all he really needed. When we are walking by faith with the Lord, we don't need to know where we are going. All we need to know is who is going with us.

As an example, many of us have had small children. You put them in the back seat. You buckle them up in their car seats. You close the back door. You get into the driver's seat. You start the car, and then you hear that question, "Mamma, Daddy, where are we going?" And if you are like me, your answer is, "It's not your business, because wherever I am going, you are going too, so just sit back and enjoy the ride." Before you start the trip, you have enough gas money to make it to your destination. You have enough food money to make it to your destination, and you have packed everything that your child will need while you are on this trip. Well, since we expect our children to surrender and ride with us by faith while we are taking care of them, why is it so difficult for us to walk with God by faith when He has been taking care of us since the day we were born? Abraham did not know where he was going, but he did know who was going with him. He knew that he had the divine protection of the Almighty God. The Lord spoke, and Abraham walked. The Lord said *left*, and Abraham started traveling East. The Lord said *right*, and

Abraham started traveling West. The Lord said *straight*, and Abraham started traveling North. Abraham did not know where he was going, but he did know at least three things about the place. He knew that it was a place of *promise*. God had given him His Word. He knew that it was a place already *prepared*. The inheritance was just waiting for his arrival. He knew it was a place of *plenty*. You need more land for a nation than you do for a family. And the Lord did not promise to make him a great family, but a great nation. We will never receive our surplus until we learn the importance of surrender.

The bigger the risk, the bigger the reward.

CHAPTER 5

I Don't Mind Waiting on the Lord

Hebrews 11:9–10
Surrender

One of the greatest mistakes Christians make in our responsibility to surrender to the Lord comes in assuming that having faith in God automatically means that our troubles and difficulties will vanish away overnight. We have become inculcated with what I like to call a microwave mentality, and we think that what we want from God should be instantly poured out into our lives. We want right-now results. And in our minds, we have partnered with Burger King in adopting the philosophy of not only wanting to "have it our way," but we also want to have it at our set time. Many of us make this assumption because we have heard so many promises of instant miracles, at-once blessings, overnight successes, get-rich-quick schemes, on-the-spot debt cancelation, and instantaneous overflow. But we need to be mindful that the Lord is not obligated to work on our timetable, because His plans for our lives are, in many instances diametrically opposite from our plans for our lives. And if you are thinking that the Lord owes you an immediate solution to your dilemma, nothing could be farther from the truth.

Now I will be the first to admit that there are times when the Lord does show up and manifest His presence and His power in our lives in an immediate fashion. But we need to remember that most of those cases are the exceptions and not the rule. Even when we read about the miracles of Jesus in the Gospels of Matthew, Mark, Luke, and John, on the surface there appears to be a whole lot of instant healing and deliverance. But when we examine the Bible closely, we discover some amazing facts: the widow at Nain had a dead husband and a dead son before Jesus ever showed up. Jairus's daughter was already dead when Jesus arrived at his house. Lazarus had been dead for four days before Jesus even showed up at the home of Mary and Martha. The woman with the issue of blood waited for twelve years before her healing came when she touched the hem of Jesus's garment. The woman who was bent over from her spirit of infirmity had been in her condition for eighteen years before she heard Jesus say, "Woman, thou art loosed." The lame man by the pool had been in his condition for thirty-eight years before Jesus healed him. Moses was on the back side of the desert for forty years before the Lord sent him back to Pharaoh with the message of "let my people go." And the blind man in John Chapter 9 had been in his condition since he was born before Jesus gave him the ability to see. The lame man in Acts Chapter 3, had been in his condition from his mother's womb before he heard Peter say, "In the name of Jesus Christ of Nazareth, rise up and walk." Not all miracles are instant and overnight in their manifestation in our lives.

> We need to learn to trust in the revelation of the promise of God even before we see the manifestation of the power of God.

Anybody can believe after it is done. But can we trust God even before we see it with our natural eyes? In the previous verse of Hebrews Chapter 11, we read about how the Lord spoke to Abraham, and he obeyed even though he did not know where he was going or how long the trip would take. Have you not taken the time to consider that it is not hard to wait for a day or two, or a week or two, because the truth of the matter is, those time frames don't represent faith? They simply represent patience. We can be patient with the mechanic who does not finish our car repairs on time. We can be patient with the contractor who does not finish our home repairs on time. But surrender to God and faith in God must include believing that God will do what He has promised to do and believing when He has not even given us a set date for the completion of the project and the miracle in our lives. When it comes to this matter of developing our faith in God, we must get to a point where we learn how to do at least three specific things. **First of all,** we must obey the Lord explicitly and completely, not just those things that we can understand. We must obey Him even when we cannot understand Him. *Secondly,* we must trust God to do what He has said He would do. We have to learn how to speak our miracle even before the miracle becomes a reality. *Thirdly,* we must learn how to wait on the Lord, and no matter how dark and dismal conditions may become, don't ever take matters into our own hands because we will only make the situation worse.

Allow me to give you a definition of faith that the Lord shared with me while I was preparing the chapter that you are now reading. "Faith is when we move out of our comfort zones to do something that will place ourselves at risk but bring glory to God." This is complete surrender to the Word of God, the Will of God, and the Way of God. If you would be honest, you would have to admit that the main reason many people are hesitant about walking with the Lord by faith is because it will require for them to do something that will not fit into their narrow way of thinking.

And before I move into the meat of this chapter, I want to quote a scripture, make a statement, and ask a question. In Genesis Chapter 12 and verse 3, we read these words that the Lord spoke to Abraham: "I will bless those who bless you, and I will curse him who curses you. **And in you all the families of the earth shall be blessed.**" Now the last part of the verse helped me to understand that we are blessed because Abraham used his faith and totally surrendered to the Lord. So now I need to ask the question, how many people around us are not being blessed, because we are failing to use our faith and totally surrender to the Lord? When we were preparing to build our Family Life Center in 2010, there were some people who thought it was too lofty of a project. But now that every one of the classrooms in that building are filled to capacity with students, I am forced to ask myself, how many children would not have a classroom for Sunday School or a gymnasium for their activities if I had not used my faith and surrendered to the Lord by leading our congregation into building the Family Life Center?

It is right here in Hebrews 11:9–10 that the writer gives us some of the extended details of how Abraham used and expressed his faith in God.

Verse 9 says, "By faith he dwelt in the land of promise as in a foreign country…" Now let me tell you what this verse really means. Abraham dwelt in this land, without building a house or owning any property other than a place for him to be buried, because he knew that this was not God's final place where he would spend eternity. This helped me understand that faith and surrender will lead us to:

I: The Unfamiliar Circumstances

Abraham did not mind moving to a new location because he knew that his move had been commanded by God, and he was also comforted by God. If we can figure out how we are doing what we are doing for God, it is not an act of faith and surrender. Instead, it is simply an act of going along with the Lord for the ride. Faith will cause us to say some things we have never said before, and we will do some things we have never done before. We will give some money at a level where we have never given before. We will take on some challenges that we have never faced before, and we will go some places that we have never gone before.

Every time we see an example of faith in the Bible, it reveals people doing what seem to be crazy, irrational, and extraordinary things, like:

- Walking across a Red Sea with a wall of water on both sides of you
- Marching around a wall seven times and then starting to shout as the wall falls down
- Going into a fiery furnace and coming out not even smelling like smoke
- Going into a den of lions and then sleeping on their manes and not being eaten by wild animals
- Praying while you are in the belly of a great fish, and the Lord allows you to be vomited up on dry land
- Going to fight a nine-foot tall giant when you are only five foot two and fifteen years old

If we are truly surrendered to the Lord, it will allow us to face and conquer some unfamiliar circumstances. Most of us want to remain in the safe areas, in the territory of the familiar, but the Lord is trying to get us to move because there are people who need to learn how to trust in the Lord by watching us. There just may be somebody who works with you, lives with you, or shops where you shop who needs to know that life is filled with ups and downs, pitfalls and difficulties, and seasons of exaltation and seasons of humiliation. There will be days of sunshine and days of rain. Somebody needs to know that there will be periods of plenty and periods of scarcity in all of our lives. But through it all, God is faithful, reliable, and trustworthy, and God will never allow our faith in Him to go unrewarded.

There were some people who looked at Abraham, and they also learned that God's promises are not always instant in their manifestation. And if you don't believe me, just look at the next part of the verse. It goes on to say, "dwelling in tents with Isaac and Jacob..." This brings to our attention that Abraham not only had the faith to handle his unfamiliar circumstances, but he also shows us how he was willing to deal with some:

II: Uncomfortable Conditions

The verse says "he was dwelling in tents." Now this almost caused me to have a Holy Ghost fit. I see at least three things here about how the Lord desires to develop our faith. First of all, the Lord did not surround him with *luxury.* He was living in tents. He was not living in a palace but in tents. This helped me understand that walking with the Lord by faith does not mean that life will be filled with all the creature comforts. There will be some sacrifice involved. Then I also took note of the fact, that there was an "s" on tent, making it plural. This means that Abraham had to change his *location,* even after he got to the land of Promise. Here is what I am trying to get you to understand. You may be in the right land by being a member of the right church, but you need to change your location and move your tent.

Let me if I can really drive home my point of emphasis here by using some geographical images. Many people need to move from Do-Nothing Drive to Commitment Court, from Robbing Road to Tithing Trail, from Passivity Path to Shouting Street, or from Aggravated Avenue to Hallelujah Highway. They need to change their location from Burden

Boulevard to Loving Lane. But the reason some of us don't want to move is because moving means that we must walk off from our old tent and relocate to a new tent, and we have become comfortable in the tent where we are living right now.

Abraham had the kind of faith that helped him to understand that he did not need luxury. He did not mind changing his location and it was all because he was leaving a *legacy* of faith for his son and his grandson to follow. If you don't believe me, just look at the verse one more time. The Bible says, he was "dwelling in tents with Isaac and Jacob..." Now this does not mean that they lived in the tents at the same time. But it does mean that Isaac learned how to walk with God by faith and how to surrender to the will of God by watching his father, and Jacob learned how to walk by faith because of what his grandfather taught his father. Let me take a shout break right here!

And I need to ask the question, are our children learning how to walk with God by faith and how to deal with their uncomfortable conditions by watching us press our way and remain committed to God even when we don't feel like it? Or do they think that things have to be luxurious, comfortable, and perfect with an iPad, iPod, iTablet, and an iPhone before they can serve the Lord? Do our children think that they need a pair of three-hundred-dollar Lebron James tennis shoes before they can shout? Do they think that faith only works on Sunday morning and that the Lord is not worthy of Bible study, Sunday school, Lord's Supper, being involved in a ministry, or, extending a helping hand to somebody who is less fortunate than they are? There will be times in the lives of all God's children when He will lead us into some uncomfortable conditions, so we need to ask ourselves if we are up for the challenge.

There is also some additional information for us to glean from right here in this same verse. It ends by saying, they were "the heirs with him of the same promise." This helps us to see his:

III: Unfailing Commitment

Now this point will be short and sweet. This part of the verse helped me understand that Isaac and Jacob never would have received their part of the inheritance if Abraham had not walked with the Lord by faith. This forced me to ask myself how many promises from God I have denied my children and grandchildren because of my lack of faith, failure to surrender, and my irresponsible behavior. I know that you have dotted every "i," crossed every "t," and every time you get home from work and church, you hang your halo up in your closet and put your wings in a secure place. I want you to know as you are reading this book that I have made some mistakes in my life. I am not proud of, them but I do not hesitate to share that truth with you if my honesty can prevent you from the mistake of failing to surrender to the Lord completely. But I also thank God for when the Word of God brought my mistakes to my attention, and I started to do everything that I could to make sure that I was doing my very best to set a good example for my children and grandchildren. I want my life to be a godly example to the people that I give spiritual leadership to. I want every person who crosses my path to pattern after my example as they walk by faith with the Lord! I shout because I want them to learn how to shout. I lift holy hands, because I want them to learn how to praise the Lord. Abraham had the kind of faith to wait on the Lord. He dealt with some *unfamiliar circumstances*, he endured some *uncomfortable conditions*, and he had an *unfailing commitment* to set the right kind of example for his son and his grandson.

Finally, verse 10 says, "For he waited for the city which has foundations, whose builder and maker is God." This represents his:

IV: Unshakable Confidence

Abraham knew that the land of Canaan was not all that the Lord had for him. And we need to get to a point where we realize that whatever we have now is not all that the Lord has for us. Abraham had the right kind of *determination*. He knew that he was not always going to be living in tents.

He was looking for a city with the right *development*. It had foundations; there was nothing shaky or unstable about it.

It was a city that was *divine*. God is the builder and maker of this city. I have confidence in God that I have another home beyond Fort Worth or any place I may live here on planet earth. You can have that same level of confidence, and it begins with a new level of faith in God and total surrender to the Word, way, and will of God.

CHAPTER 6

THE DEVELOPMENT BEHIND MY DIFFICULTY

St. John 16:33
SURRENDER

There are times in all of our lives when we are going through seasons of difficulty and find ourselves having more questions than answers, more pain than relief, and more fears than comfort. During those times, when we seem to be overwhelmed and engulfed by cataclysmic and catastrophic situations that are beyond our control, we need to redirect our focus. I want to recommend that we make a conscious effort to mentally and faithfully move away from what is causing us to feel defeated and start focusing on the One who is able to help us to rise above our fears, press our way through our pain, and remain faithful and committed even when we don't know why we are going through what we are going through. I have discovered that whatever God does and whatever He allows, He has a purpose behind it and the purpose is bigger than our pain. One of the things that has helped me to place all of my problems in their proper perspective is when I embrace the truth and come to the realization that God's purpose for my life is bigger than the problems that I am going through.

Whatever we deal with as Christians as it relates to our representation of Jesus Christ is designed to bring Him all the glory. One of the main reasons modern Christians have so much difficulty processing this truth is because we do not define trouble and tribulations as the Bible defined it when it was written. We call one thing trouble, and the Bible is speaking about something completely different when it defines trouble. Let me give you a few illustrations about what I am referring to. If I were to ask any audience where I was preaching or teaching to raise their hands if they have had or are presently facing some major troubles and tribulations in their lives right now, I am sure that hands would be lifted all over the place. I would make a follow up statement like this: "**Okay, now listen very carefully to my next question.** Let me see the hands of you who have had some major troubles in your life because people were out to defeat you and physically harm you only because of the strength of your relationship with Jesus Christ and your total commitment to keep living by the commandments in His Word in the midst of hostile environments?"

I am trying to focus on how much of our trouble in our lives is related exclusively to our commitment to the Lord. Here is what I am trying to get you to understand. Most of the stuff that we call tribulations and troubles are really nothing more than personal drama, self-imposed hardships, and worldly worry.

> **Most of the stuff that keeps us awake at night and causes us to have lives filled with frustration is based on the poor choices we have made without directions from God's Word.**

The things that we call tribulations in many instances have little to nothing to do with our representation or our relationship with Jesus Christ. (Let that soak in for a few minutes while you think about your troubles.)

Did you not know that whenever the Bible speaks about trouble, it was always in reference to people's lives being threatened because of their connection to the Lord and His church? I don't think that you are getting it, so, let me blow your mind and put it back together again right here. When the Bible talks about how we should handle our problems, tribulations, and difficulties, it was not talking about baby daddy drama or having baby mama drama with your boyfriend's ex-girlfriend. It is

THE DEVELOPMENT BEHIND MY DIFFICULTY

not the drama of catching your boyfriend with another woman. It is not drama that comes when your income tax check did not come on time so your lights were turned off.

When James said, "Count it all joy when you go through diverse temptations," he was not talking about when your child did not get the scholarship to Yale and somebody else's child, whom you feel was not as deserving, did. He was not talking about when somebody else at your job got the promotion, and you were overlooked for the third time. He was not talking about when the man you were shacking with left when you got pregnant, and he moved and started shacking with somebody else because you could no longer take care of him as this new woman will.

These things did not even exist when these verses were written. These verses in the Bible about holding on in the midst of trouble were designed to strengthen the faith of people who were doing everything they could to live for Jesus but were still being hacked to death, boiled in hot oil, and crucified upside down; their homes were being burned to the ground; their children were being raped and murdered; they were cast into prison; they were being stabbed to death and beaten with rods; and they were being placed on guillotines and their heads were being chopped off. They were not just losing jobs and going through a period where people were talking behind their backs. NO, NO! These people were experiencing real trouble, unlike anything most of us will ever have to deal with during our lifetimes.

So when Jesus speaks these words to His disciples here in this text, He was not just preparing them to deal with devilish deacons, tricky trustees, unruly ushers, cantankerous choir members, nasty nurses, mean men's ministry members, worrisome women, and profiteering preachers. All these things were minor, miniscule, insipid, trivial, insignificant, and petty in comparison to what they were about to face. When Jesus spoke these words here in John Chapter 16, it is a part of what scholars call the upper-room discourse. He was informing His *disciples* that He was getting ready for His *death*, which would be followed by His **deposit** into the grave. Then He would be *delivered* from the grave, and finally He would make His *departure* to go back home to His Father. Now, in the midst of His death, His deposit, His deliverance, and His departure, He did not want them to become distracted by the difficulties that the devil would throw in their direction. So He speaks these words to them here in this text. He says, "These things I have spoken to you, that in Me you may have peace." If we are going to be able to experience the Lord's development during our difficulties, we need to have the faith to maintain:

I: Confidence in His Word

Notice carefully what Jesus says: "I have spoken these things to you for a specific reason." And did you not know that many of us have not been able to properly evaluate what real trouble is, from what is only personal drama, because we do not pay close enough attention to the Word of God? Have you not taken the time to consider that our grief is temporary, transitory, and only a testing period in our lives? But to the contrary, His Word is eternal, everlasting, and perpetual. His Word has withstood the test of time. Water cannot drown it, fire can't burn it, bombs can't blast it, undertakers can't bury it, time cannot outlast it, and the devil cannot destroy it. This is the Lord's way of making us aware that the only thing that will get us through our trouble and allow us to rise to every challenge that we are confronted with is our knowledge and confidence in His Word. Jesus says, "These things I have spoken." The "en" on end of the word "spoke," lets me know that He was making reference to some things that He had already said. This forces us to ask ourselves what we are doing while the Lord is speaking. In many of our churches, we have people in attendance who are busy and preoccupied with things like texting, e-mailing, sleeping, lusting, walking, daydreaming, and maybe just ignoring. Whatever has demanded our attention away from the Word of God will cause a time when we will regret that we were not paying close attention to what the Lord was speaking through His human vessel.

Look at this verse one more time. Jesus does not say, "These things I have *done for you,* that in Me you may have peace." No, He says, "these things *I have spoken* to you that in Me you may have peace." This helped me understand that my real peace is not based on what the Lord has done for me, but on what the Lord has said to me. (Insert shout here!) He says, "In Me, you may have peace." The key to finding real peace comes in knowing that we are living in Him and He is living in us. When my soul is weary and my eyes are filled with tears, I don't need the Lord to give me a new suit, a new car, or a new pair of shoes, but I need Him to speak to my heart and tell me, "I will never leave you nor forsake you." When my enemies are tying to cancel everything that I am striving to do for the Lord and to His glory, I don't need a new relationship or a new job. I need Him to speak to my heart and tell me, "Fret not thyself because of evil doers, neither be thou envious against the workers of iniquity, for they shall soon but cut down like the green grass." I'm simply trying to make us cognizant of the truth that His Word will hold us even when our stuff leaves us, but our stuff will never satisfy us, if we don't have His Word.

Jesus goes on in verse 33 to say, "In the world you will have tribulation." This moved me from a level of confidence in His Word to a position of becoming mentally:

II: Conscious of the World

And this is just a fancy way of saying, get ready, because trouble is going to come. Now this is where many of us are caught off guard. We allow trouble to sneak up on us, as opposed to us being ready for the inevitableness of trouble. We need to be constantly mindful that it does not matter how holy, righteous, fine, handsome, ugly, broke, rich, nice, or mean you are, trouble is going to come. Now just in case you may be wondering if there is any difference between a Christian having trouble and an ungodly person having trouble, the answer is yes. Ungodly people have to face their troubles by relying on artificial substances like crack, cocaine, Prozac, valium, Jack Daniels, Budweiser, Miller, margaritas, marijuana, and Crown Royal, and all of those things are either illegal or extremely costly. But Christians can face their troubles with prayer, worship, praise, Bible study, personal devotion, revivals, conferences, ministry involvement, and fasting, and all of these things are legal and are free. Jesus wants us to be aware that the devil will attack us, and we will face trouble in our lives, but we will never have to face it all by ourselves. Take a moment to just throw your arms around yourself and say to yourself, "I ain't in this all by myself."

If we are going to discover the importance of truly surrendering to the Lord, we cannot overlook the importance of developing a greater level of confidence in His Word, and we also need to be conscious of this world in which we live.

But finally, the verse ends by saying, "But be of good cheer, I have overcome the world." It is here that we hear Jesus giving us some heavenly advice about the:

III: Cheerfulness of Our Worship

He is saying to us that no matter what the devil throws in our direction, we shouldn't dare allow it stop our praise. Jesus uses the word "but." In Mrs. Johnson's second grade English class, we learned that this word is a conjunction, which means what I am about to say is going to be different from what I have already said. In other words, I have told you that you will have trouble, BUT, be of good cheer and let you cheer overshadow your conflicts. This was a phrase that Jesus used on several occasions. In Matthew Chapter 9 verse 2, He gives us the good cheer of His pardon. In Matthew Chapter 9 verse 22, He gives us the good cheer of His power. In Matthew Chapter 14 verse 27, He gives us the good cheer of His presence. And here in John Chapter 16, verse 33, He gives us the good cheer of His promise. And when we have His pardon, power, presence, and promise, there is but one thing left for us to do, and that is to give Him the praise. This phrase "good cheer" means to take courage, which lets me know that I don't have to be worried about what the devil will throw in my direction, and I don't have to be timid in my praise.

All of my difficulties are being used by God to help me to develop into all that the Lord desires for me to be. Don't run from your trouble. Shout your way through your trouble. When we totally surrender to Him and His will for our lives, He will fight battles and defeat enemies for us that we would never be able to handle on our own.

CHAPTER 7

CAN JESUS USE YOUR HOUSE?

Matthew 26:17–20
SURRENDER

I never cease to be amazed that God's Word remains pregnant with new truth and continues to give birth to fresh revelations each time we read it and hear it preached or taught. Did you not know that God's Word is free from a posture of being stale, stagnant, and melancholy? There are times when people will make the statement that they are not being helped and developed by reading the Bible, and my response to them is, "The problem is not with the Bible; the problem just may be that you are not reading it often enough." We make the mistake of wanting to go to God's Word and read a verse or two during our times of frustration for a quick fix, and we never return to it until a new problem arises. But the Word of God should be a part of our daily lives. There should never be a day that goes by when a Christian does not read something from the Word of God. I have discovered that when I read it on a regular basis, I don't have to try to cram a whole lot in when a crisis arises in my life.

Here in the Gospel of St. Matthew, we find new insight on an old story, and it provides for us some practical and portable principles to prepare ourselves to walk in the path of the Lord and fulfill our purpose as children of the most high God. The Lord is still working with and working through human personalities in order to accomplish His plans here on planet Earth. The Lord has chosen to share His will for the lives of people by using those of us who are saved, sealed, sanctified, and secure in our relationships with Him. The Lord wants each one of us to know that whatever we have, He has given it to us. Whatever positive goals we have accomplished are only because of His grace and mercy. He has favored us, fathered us, forgiven us, and been faithful to us. Many of us are walking in the promises of God and are enjoying His blessings, provisions, and protection. Yet we are not making ourselves available for Him to use us at the same level where He has showered His abundance upon our lives. Have you not taken the time to consider that the Lord has kept us in good health, and He has assigned angels to serve as our guardians both day and night? The Lord has made our enemies leave us alone. He has kept us from losing our minds, and He has surrounded us with people who have a desire to encourage our hearts during times of grief and bereavement. He has been loving enough to meet our needs even before we knew that the need ever existed.

Right here in this story we find Jesus preparing Himself for the ultimate fulfillment of His pilgrimage here on planet Earth. He has spent better than three years of His life healing the sick, raising the dead, feeding the hungry, giving sight to the blind, and forgiving the guilty. Now, He is about to take some time to give His disciples some intricate details of what is about to happen in the next few hours and over the next three days. He does not want them to be caught off guard with the events about to transpire. So He decides to disconnect Himself from the masses and spend some time in private with these twelve men who have been following Him for the past three years.

In verse 17, we are told that it was the first day of the Feast of the Unleavened Bread. This was a feast that all Jews celebrated as they reflected on how the Lord had delivered their forefathers out of the hand of the evil despot and tyrannical ruler by the name of pharaoh and out of the land of Egypt. We are also told that Jesus's disciples came to Him and asked Him where He wanted them to prepare for Him to eat the Passover. And I think that this would be a good time for me to ask how interested are you in making some preparations for Jesus to be comfortable? Most of us are only interested in making preparations for ourselves. But these men wanted to have things prepared for Jesus.

Notice carefully in this story what Jesus tells them to do in verse 18. He says, "Go into the city to a certain man, and say to him, 'The Teacher says, "My time is at hand, I will keep the Passover at your house with My disciples."''' Then we read something remarkable in verses 19 and 20. The disciples did what they were told to do. They prepared the Passover at this man's house, and only twelve of them plus Jesus were a part of the feast. In other words, this man allowed Jesus and His disciples to use his house, and he did not even have a chance to eat or to share in any of the feasting activities, because the text clearly states in verse 20, that Jesus sat down with the twelve.

So this is why I raise the question in this chapter. Can Jesus use your house without you feeling like you have to receive something in return? We do not even know who this "certain man" was, but we do know that he must have been somebody who knew Jesus and did not mind allowing Jesus to use what he had whenever the Master needed to use it. Luke gives us even greater details in his gospel. He tells us that Jesus told Peter and John that they would find a man who was carrying a pitcher of water. They were told to follow him, and he would make his home available. I wanted to know what was it about this man that caused him to give his home to Jesus for this meal, and he did not even had the privilege to share in any of the festivities or eat any of the food. So I prayed and asked the Lord what it was that He wanted me to share with His people about giving our most prized and precious possessions over to Him without feeling like we deserved something in return. I hope you will agree with me when I say that for most people, our homes are our most valuable asset. We will not allow just anybody to come into our homes, let alone use our home for a meal when we are not there to supervise the affair. I was really interested in discovering what was it that led this man into making such a bold move and what lessons does the Lord what the rest of us who need to surrender to Him to learn from this episode. As a result of my interest, my head almost exploded when the Lord shared these principles with me.

The first thing I see in this text is what I want to call this man's:

I: Respect for the Representatives of Jesus

Notice carefully, if you will, that Jesus did not ask this man to use his house. He sent His disciples to ask him on His behalf. This is the problem that many of us have in our relationships with the Lord: we are not too fond of the people that He chooses to use to represent Him. These were not perfect men. If you don't believe me, let me call the roll. There was doubting Thomas in this group. Cussing, denying Peter was in this group. Skeptic Nathanial was in this group. Embezzling Matthew was in this group. And egotistical James and John were in this group. Some of us would have allowed Jesus to use our homes, but we never would have allowed these flawed and frail disciples to come into our place of residence. But this was not the case with this homeowner. He did not question these men, and he did not say, "If Jesus wants to use my house, let Him come and ask me Himself." He did not ask, "How long will you need my house?" He did not ask, "How much are you going to pay me to lease my house?" All this man does is make his house available for Jesus and His disciples to use.

Many people in the body of Christ fail to realize that whenever their pastoral leader stands before them to make a special request, all he is doing is asking them to make available to the Lord what they have that He desires to use. But the main reason people don't respond is because we have too many personality conflicts with the people that the Lord uses to make His requests. We feel like the Lord owes us a personal explanation. This man simply respected the men who were representing Jesus. Our churches will never be all that God desires for them to be until we learn the importance of honoring those who are in positions of spiritual authority over us. Paul says we should "esteem them very highly for their works sake."

Evidently, this man was so willing because He had heard Jesus speak through other human vehicles before. But many of us want to pick and choose what we will listen to from the Lord's spokesmen. We will gladly receive it when the man or woman of God says something that will benefit us, but we will reject it when the man or woman of God informs us that the Lord is requiring something from us that we consider to be near and dear to our hearts.

Then in verse 19, we read these words: "So the disciples did as Jesus had directed them, and they prepared the Passover." Here, we see how this man:

II: Responded to the Request from Jesus

Now, I am sure that you will agree with me when I say that we have many people in the church who will show what I want to call "polite respect" to their spiritual leadership. The only problem is they never do what the Lord has commanded them to do. They are not disrespectful, rude, or mean; they just hear the Word and after the benediction, go on about their business without making any changes or any sacrifices in their lives. But according to the text, this man respected the representatives of Jesus and he responded to the request of Jesus. What will the Lord need to do for you to respond to what He is saying?

Allow me paint this picture for you to present my point more vividly. One of the quietest moments in most African American worship experiences is after the welcome at an afternoon service. The program calls for a response, and no one comes up to say anything. Then the preacher has to say two or three times, "Can we get a response, please?" Well, I have come to tell you that the Lord wants to use what you have, and He wants some of your most valuable possessions. Now, can I get a response, please?

> **The Lord needs more people to be active in ministry, stop taking the easy way out, and help other people to grow in their relationship with Jesus Christ. Now, can I get a response, please?**

The Lord wants people to be committed, sacrificial, loyal, devoted, dedicated, excited, motivated, prepared, and energetic. Now, can I get a response, please? Most of us make the mistake of thinking that the preacher is always talking to and about somebody else when it comes to this matter of responding. But I have come to tell everyone that this is a message for all of us. Have you not taken the time to consider that if this man would not have made his home available, Jesus would not have had a place to eat the Passover with His disciples? Now some of you may be saying, "Now wait a minute, pastor. This is Jesus, and surely He could have used somebody else's house." And that is exactly where the problem lies. We always want the Lord to use somebody else's time, money, energy, influence, gifts, and sacrifices. But I thank God that this man did not have this kind of attitude. If you are a member of a church family, there is a strong possibility that the reason you are able to worship in the beautiful sanctuary where you worship is because others before you allowed the Lord to use their financial resources, and some of them have gone home to be with the Lord. But they made the sacrifice for all of our conveniences.

Finally, we see how this man:

III: Released His Resources to Jesus

He allowed Jesus to use his home. And for most of us, our homes, and our places of residence are our most valuable possessions. Now, notice carefully what *I did not* say. I did not say this man allowed Jesus to *have his home*. I also did not title this sermon, "Can Jesus *have* your home?" And the reason I did not ask that question is Jesus does not need a permanent place of residence here on earth. He already has that in heaven. In other words, if we will allow Him to use our possessions and our homes here on earth, He will give us a home in heaven. Look again at verse 20. We are told that when the evening time had come, Jesus sat down with the twelve. And in verse 21, we are told that they started eating.

Now let me use my sanctified stretchability right here! (I know that's not a word, but you get my point.) I believe that this man said to Jesus, "I am not going to limit you to just one room. Whatever space You need, my house is Your house. Lord, I have already gone to the grocery store, and tell your disciples, they don't have to shop for any herbs, garlic, leeks, onions, bread, wine, or even an unspotted lamb. Because when they told me that *You* were coming, I got everything in order." This final revelation almost brought tears to my eyes.

This man, in our text, was not Jairus, whose daughter Jesus had healed.

This man was not the brother to the woman with the issue of blood.

This was not blind Bartimaeus.

This was not the centurion with the sick servant.

This was not the man with the withered hand.

This was not the man who ran out of wine at his wedding feast.

This was not the man who was let down through the roof by his friends.

This was not the man whom Jesus had cast demons from while he was living in the graveyard.

This was not the man whose son was sick, and Jesus healed him because His disciples could not do it.

Maybe you are wondering why I mentioned all those men. Those men would have allowed the Lord to use their homes because Jesus had done something for them. But this man allowed Jesus to use his home, not because of what He had done, but because of who He was. And this is where I want to conclude this first segment of this book by asking you when will you learn how to give the Lord your best, not because of what He has done, but because of who He is? He is our Creator, our Savior, and our Comforter. He made us, He saved us, and He is keeping us. He deserves the right to use whatever He asks us for.

Oh, and by the way, the only reason you have a house is

He gave it to you in the first place!

Service
in the
Work of the Lord

CHAPTER 8

POSING A REAL THREAT TO THE DEVIL

Acts 12:1–7
SERVICE

Get comfortable. Turn your cell phone off. If you have something pressing that you need to attend to in the next few minutes, this is not the chapter that you want to read now. This one requires your wholehearted and undivided attention because we are about to address some issues that will reveal how committed we truly are to the service of the Kingdom of God and our relationship with Jesus Christ. Still reading? Okay, let's get started.

How threatened do you think the devil is because of your relationship with Jesus Christ? Do you make him jealous when he sees how much of your time, talent, and treasure you give to God and how little you give to yourself and to him? Do you have him trembling in his blasphemous boots and shaking in his satanic shoes, or is he in a posture of dormancy because he knows that he does not have to bother you because you are not bothering him? I believe that God wants us to live the kind of committed lives for Him, and be so closely connected to Him, that it literally causes the devil to lose sleep over how many people we are taking out of his kingdom and leading into the kingdom of God. Many of us fail to realize that the Christian life is warfare. We are in a fight for the rest of our lives, because we are now friends with God, which also makes us enemies to satan.

Whenever you have an enemy, you may as well get ready to do some fighting. I believe one of the main problems we have in this area of our lives lies in the fact that many people have received misinformation concerning what the Christian life is really all about. We think that once we accept Jesus Christ as our personal Savior, all of our troubles are going to instantly vanish away. But nothing could be farther from the truth. As a matter of fact, we may have even more battles once we surrender our lives to Jesus Christ, but the good news is once we become a child of God, we don't have to fight the battles all by ourselves. Jesus never promised that we would not have storms and difficulties in our lives, but He did promise that He would be our protection in the midst of the storm. He said to His disciples, "In this world you shall have tribulations, but be of good cheer because I have overcome the world."

When we believe in our hearts that Jesus died for our sins and confess that truth with our mouths, salvation instantly takes place in our souls. We are immediately transferred from people who were on their way to hell and become citizens of heaven. When we are saved, the devil also receives notice. It causes his heart to be filled with grief, just to know that he has lost another person whom he thought he was going to be able to use to promulgate his demoralizing, devilish, and destructive deeds. But now we have decided to make Jesus our choice. I'm trying to help you understand that the devil is always unhappy whenever a person makes up his or her mind to say no to him and yes to Jesus Christ.

At the beginning of this chapter, I posed the question: How threatened do you think the devil is because of your relationship with Jesus Christ? But now, I want to ask another thought-provoking question.

How confident do you think God is in having *you* as one of His everyday examples?

How much joy fills the heart of God when He looks at your life and sees that you are a walking, living, and breathing example of what a real Christian should look, act, and live like? Do you think the Lord is confident enough in you to tell another believer, "If you want to see what true forgiveness is, look at her life? If you want to see what real genuine stewardship is life, look at his life. If you want to know how to press your way and remain faithful to the Lord even in the midst of adverse circumstances, look at them." In other words, do you think God is comfortable in using you as one of His prime examples and displays? Many of us fail to realize that the only way we will ever become a more serious threat to the devil is for us to become more closely connected and devoted to Jesus Christ. This was the one thing that really concerned the devil about the life of the apostle Peter. The Bible tells us in Luke 22:31 that satan had a desire to sift Peter like wheat, but Jesus told him that He had prayed for him. He also said, "When you are converted, strengthen your brother." I want you to know that satan still desires to sift us. He desires to destroy us and cause us shame and embarrassment. The devil desires to cause us to abandon our families, fail our spouses with infidelity, wane in our faith, remain inactive in our church, and be known as people who are up-to-date on all the worldly gadgets and activities but be completely illiterate when it comes to the things of God.

The reason Peter was able to escape the devil's vice grip is because Jesus prayed for him. And I have come with some good news to let you know that the Lord has prayed for you also. Since Peter could be used by the Lord despite his past failures, this gives us the reassurance that the Lord can also use us despite our past failures.

When the incident recorded in Acts Chapter 12 took place, Peter was now preaching for Jesus, and more than three thousand people were being saved. All this was causing the devil some major aggravations, so he puts a plan in place in an attempt to stop Peter. The devil works through the evil personality of Herod the king of Jerusalem to cause aggravation to the Church of Jesus Christ. Herod was from a ruthless family. They were so ruthless and so hated by their own people that one of them decided to have some prominent men of the city arrested and kept in prison. He then instructed his soldiers to kill these men on the same day of his death, just to make sure that there would be some mourning in the land on the day that he died. The devil will use whomever he can to attack the people of God in an attempt to stop us from fulfilling our godly assignments. The devil put a plan in place to stop Peter.

Before we progress any further, I need to pause and ask a question: Does the devil have to put a plan in place to stop you from fulfilling your ministry? Or does he just sit by and laugh, because he knows that though you promise to do for the Lord and His church, you will never really make good those promises or commitments? Let that sink in for a moment. Are you ready to continue? Okay let's move on. I am proud of you.

In verses 2 and 3 of Acts Chapter 12, we are told that Herod killed James the brother of John, and when he saw that it pleased the Jews, he also had Peter arrested. Now I want us to notice carefully what kind of threat this man Peter was to Herod and then ask ourselves if the devil feels a need to set up this kind of attack against us. And if not, why not? In verse 4, we are told that they arrested Peter. They seized him. The devil knew that the only way he could stop Peter was to get control of him. We need to take a moment and recognize that when we seem to be shackled by a multitude of negative situations, it very well could be because the devil knows that just one or two minor sets of circumstances will not stop us. This also helps us to understand the importance of making sure that we do not abuse our spiritual freedoms in Christ. We must learn how to handle our freedom in a Godly manner because if we do not, the devil will just allow us to continue to roam free, and it will lead to greater temptation and more atrocious sinful activities. We should be living the kind of committed lives for God that cause the devil to feel like the only way he can stop us is to arrest us. Don't worry when you feel like you have been arrested by trouble. Just keep the fact in mind that Jesus has your bail money, and he has already planned for your escape.

In 1 Corinthians 10:13, we read these comforting words: "No temptation has overtaken you except such as is common to man; but God is faithful, who will not allow you to be tempted beyond what you are able, but with the temptation will also make a way of escape, that you may be able to bear it." The Lord often allows us to go into trouble just to show our enemies that they do not have the power to hold us beyond God's ability to deliver us. Just in case you may be wondering how Peter was able to handle life when the devil seized him, well, the answer is found at the end of verse 5. While Peter was in jail, the church was praying for him. This reveals an extremely important principle. Peter was committed to the church, and they were praying for him when he needed them, because he had been there for them when they needed him.

> **Many contemporary Christians want their local churches to pray for them and come to their assistance during difficult times when the church is needed, but they are nowhere to be found when their churches need them.**

Then in verse 4, we also discover how the enemy surrounded him. Peter was such a threat to Herod that Herod felt he needed to assign four squads of soldiers to stand guard over him. When the Bible says "four squads of soldiers," this means there were some sixteen men who had the responsibility of making sure that Peter remained in prison. Two men were chained to him. There was one on his right and one on his left. There were two other soldiers who stood on the outside of the jail to make sure no one came in and no one left out without proper authorization. These men would change shifts every six hours. How many soldiers do you think the devil has to assign to the majority of Christian believers today to keep them from doing what they should be doing for Jesus Christ? The sad truth is, we will press our way through many obstacles to do things that will benefit us personally and then give up so easily when we face a roadblock in fulfilling our Christian responsibilities. But this was not the case with Peter. Herod not only put Peter in prison, but he also did everything he knew how to do to keep him in prison.

This part of the story ends with some great news. We discover that when we have given the Lord our very best, He will be there when we need Him the most. The Bible tells us that Herod *seized* Peter. The soldiers *secured* Peter. But only God had the power to *set Peter free.* In verse 6 of Acts Chapter 12, the Bible tells us that Herod was about to bring Peter out. That phrase, "bring him out," means that Herod was about to kill him. That night, Peter was sleeping! Did you read that? Peter was about to be killed, and here he is sleeping. How on earth was he able to sleep knowing that he was less than twenty-four hours from being killed? When you know that God has your life in His hands, then you can go on to bed and get a good night's sleep because the Lord will show up just when we need Him the most. Zoom in real close. Every believer needs to know that our lives are totally in God's hands, and however He chooses to resolve our trouble, either permanently or temporarily, will all work for our good.

I want you to notice some of the events in this text that literally blew my mind. While Peter was *sleeping,* an angel of the Lord *stood* by him. A light started *shining* in the prison, and then the angel *struck* Peter on the side and raised him up. The angel *spoke* to Peter and told him to "arise quickly." And his *shackles* fell off. The Lord had *set* him free. You missed it! All of this happened with two soldiers chained to him and two other soldiers standing outside of the prison. They did not even know that Peter was gone until the next day. This helped me understand that only God has the power to *deliver* us from our enemies without *disturbing* our enemies There are times when God will leave our enemies in place so that they can help us to testify about how God brought us out when they tried to hold us down. And I just believe that if we know that God has delivered us, we should be a threat to the devil. We should be threatening the devil by:

I: Walking in Our Purpose

Make up your mind today to start doing more for God than you have ever done before.

II: Giving Him our Possessions

Everything we have has come from God. We need to wake up every morning with this question on our minds: What shall I render to the Lord for all of His benefits toward me? If you know that God has been good to you, you ought to honor Him with the first fruits of your labor.

III: Lifting Him in Praise

The angel told Peter in verse 7 to arise quickly! If we are going to be a threat to the devil, we need to do it right now! Procrastination is not a threat to him, but a passionate and persistent pursuit to walk in your purpose will cause the devil to really feel threatened by your relationship with the Lord. Let's make up our minds to make him jealous when he sees the love Jesus has for us and the love and commitment that we have for the Lord.

CHAPTER 9

What to Do After Your Chains Fall Off

Acts 12:7–13
Service

As sad as it is to have to admit to it, I must say that one of the major things that cripples many Christians is we have little to no idea of what is expected of us and from us after we have been delivered by Jesus Christ. Far too many people believe that once they accept the Lord as their personal Savior, they can now sit back, take it easy, and just wait for Jesus to return and take them to heaven. But the real truth of the matter is that salvation is a dualistic process with both components having equal importance. First of all, it assures us of our eternal relationship with God. Because of salvation, we no longer have to worry about suffering the penalty that we deserved because of the crimes we have committed against God. Secondly, because we are saved, it should also cause us to recognize our Godly responsibilities here on Earth. Have you taken the time to consider that God has provided for our eternity in heaven? We have streets of gold waiting for us. We have a mansion without a mortgage waiting for us. We have a tree that is good for the healing of the nations waiting for us. We have a land of no more death, disease, destruction, and devastation waiting for us. So I believe that the very least we can do is to be committed and effective workers for the Lord Jesus Christ while we spend these few years of our lives here on earth. When God delivers us and brings us out from whatever situation it may be that was holding us captive, He does it with a purpose in mind. God sets us free so that we can grow and mature into the quality kingdom citizens that He would have us to be.

> **God sets us free so that we will no longer live as prisoners to sin and act like we are convicts of the devil's demonic strongholds.**

When we carefully examine this text here in Acts Chapter 12, I need to ask you to please allow me, if you will, to add a point of clarity here. This text by no means suggests that Peter received his salvation when he was miraculously delivered by God from this jail. But it does give us some insight into this matter of Christian responsibility even after we have established a relationship with Jesus Christ. This story provides some valuable information to those of us who know that we are saved but are struggling to find our place in ministry and our purpose in the kingdom of God. I need to remind you that even after we have been saved and set free from the eternal penalty of sin, we are not immune from the pressure of sin, the presence of sin, and the pleasures of sin. The devil will do whatever he can to arrest us with his demonic traps and hold us hostage on temporary lockdown. (There is a major contrast here.)

Peter was arrested because he was preaching the gospel of Jesus Christ and was healing people in the name of Jesus. But to the contrary, many of us are held captive by the devil, because we decided to go to him and turn ourselves in by just surrendering to his evil schemes. The devil did not even have to put out a warrant for the arrest of some of us. We just walked up to his prison and said, "Here I am. Go ahead and lock me up." We do this by becoming incarcerated by poor habits, bad relationships, and a failure to remain connected to the Lord, which automatically allows us to be susceptible to the schemes and tricks of the devil.

I believe that we should live the kinds of lives that pose a threat to the devil. Instead of us volunteering to work for him, he should be jealous because of how much time, energy, and influence we are using for the Lord. In the previous chapter, we read about Peter's incarceration by Herod and the plans he had to kill him after the Passover celebration was complete. But God miraculously stepped in and altered the devil's plans. He sent an angel to awaken Peter, and immediately his chains fell off. Notice if you will that the Lord sends an *angel* to deliver Peter. This word angel is *"angelos"* in Greek, and it means a messenger or a pastor. Did you not know that the Lord sends His preachers to pulpits every Sunday all over this world because He knows that some of His people need to be delivered?

You may not be in a prison with barbed wire and armed guards. People are in different kinds of prison. They need deliverance from a bad habit, an unhealthy relationship, or a mean disposition. They need to be delivered from an idle posture in the church, a foul mouth, a lying tongue, or a lustful eye. Some people need to be delivered from a lack of commitment. Whatever it is, the good news is that the bail has already been paid, Jesus is your defense attorney, God is the judge, and all of the charges have been dropped. The Lord now wants you to know that you can walk in the kind of freedom that He had planned for you when He saved you. Verse 8 of this text helps us to understand one of the things we must do when God has set us free, and if we fail to do it, we could wind up right back in the prison all over again.

The Bible tells us that the angel said to Peter, "Gird yourself and tie your sandals; put on your garment, and follow me." And notice that Peter did everything that he was told to do. He exhibited:

I: Detailed Obedience

When the angel told Peter to put on everything he had when he went into the prison, I believe this was the Lord's way of making us aware of the need to listen attentively to His representative so that we can remain free once He has set us free. I also believe this is the Lord's way of making us aware that if we go in correctly, we cannot also come out with everything we had before we went in. If we are not careful, we will begin to make our own decisions, follow our own whims, and heed the advice of anybody and everybody who crosses our paths. In verse 9, we are told that Peter did not completely understand it was the angel of the Lord speaking to him, but he thought that he may have been seeing a vision. When God delivers us from a terrible situation, He knows that it is very easy for us to quickly lose our way. Peter was told to put on his clothes, which lets us know that maybe he was about to be exposed to some inclement weather. God knows what we need to have on before we attempt to leave our incarcerated situation. As believers, we need to put on the whole armor of God so that we may be able to stand against the tricks of the devil.

Peter was also told to tie up his shoes. This helped me understand that wherever we are right now is not where God wants us to remain. When you put on your shoes, it is a sign that you are about to move to a new location. He was told to also put on his outer garment, and finally the angel said, "Follow me." Now, notice if you will, the angel does not explain anything to Peter. All he does is give instructions and commands to Peter. I think I may need to repeat that, because too many of us want the Lord to give us an explanation when all God has promised are provisions and commands.

> **Peter did not know where he was going, but he was willing to follow the angel because he believed that since the angel had gotten him out of the mess he was in, he could also keep him out of that mess.**

God uses His preachers as instruments to lead people out of their sins. But it becomes our responsibility to be mindful that the Word of God that got us out is the only thing that will also keep us out. The Word of God from the man or woman of God will provide a pathway of true spiritual freedom. Whenever you get to a point where you stop following God because it no longer seems to make sense, I'm telling you that you are headed in the wrong direction. We must make up our minds to obey all the instructions given to us from the Word of God, not just the ones that seem logical, rational, and reasonable, but all of them, even when they seem to contradict common sense.

In verse 10, there is another helpful principle brought to our attention. The angel or the messenger from God led Peter past the first and second guard post, and they came to the iron gate that led out to the city. Once they arrived there, the Bible tells us that it opened on its own accord.

There were no remote controls and automatic garage door and gate openers in those days. This was not an act of magic, this was a miracle. Men can perform magic, but only God can do the miraculous. Verse 10 goes on to tell us that they went out down one street, and the angel departed from Peter. Here we discover how Peter exercised some:

II: Personal Responsibility

The Lord sent the angel to lead Peter out of what he cannot get out of, but once he is free, the angel departs from him. I believe this is the Lord's way of informing us that He will send you a pastor, a ministry leader, or a godly friend, to help you get out of the mess you are in right now, but once you have been set free, you must accept some personal responsibility for your future actions. Your pastor or the person who led you to Christ should not have to hold your hand every day of your life once God has delivered you. You must come to a point where you can stand on your own two feet. There are always more sheep than there are shepherds. And when you keep doing the same thing over and over again to get yourself locked up, you are taking away time that the shepherd could be using to liberate sheep for their first time, and you have been delivered seven times. Now the question may be raised: Where do we go when the Lord has set us free? And the answer is found right here in this text. Verses 11 and 12 make us aware of the fact that when Peter came to himself—or when he got himself together and balanced out his equilibrium—he knew that the Lord had sent an angel to deliver him. We have this in common with Peter; we can say with boldness and with confidence that the Lord has delivered us from whatever the devil was using to hold us captive.

In verse 12, we find the key to remaining free once we have been set free. The verse says, "So, when he had considered this, he came to the house of Mary, the mother of John whose surname was Mark, where many were gathered together praying." There it is. Peter went to the place of God to gather with the people of God, who were praying to God, because he knew that he had been protected by God. When God has set you free, you need to get to church as fast as you can and come as often as you can. This is one of the reasons I have a great deal of difficulty believing people when they say that they want to remain free from the devil's destructive tactics, but they never associate with godly people and never come to church.

Let me show you what I am talking about. If you want crack, you go to the crack house. If you want to party, you go to the clubhouse. If you need education, you go to the schoolhouse; if you are guilty they put you in the jail house. And if you want to maintain your freedom, you need to get to the church house. Peter came to the place where he knew he could find at least three things.

1) The people of God. (We need to surround ourselves with godly people.)
2) The prayers to God. (We need to be in a place of prayer—a place where people are praying for us and where we can pray for others.)
3) The praise of God (Whenever God sets somebody free, there is bound to be some praise going on.)

We must come to a point where we accept some personal responsibility for maintaining our freedom.

This story has helped us to see the need to submit to the Lord with *detailed obedience*. It helps us to see the need to accept our *personal responsibility*. But then finally, verse 13 says, "And as Peter knocked at the door of the gate, a girl named Rhoda came to answer." Here we realize the need to:

III: Remain Persistent

This verse helped me understand that just because we are walking in the will of God does not mean the every door is going to automatically open to us. When the angel led Peter out of the prison, verse 10 tells us that the iron gate opened of its own accord. But here we see him standing and the door of the place where the saints have gathered, and he has to keep on knocking. There will be times when we may come to the house of the Lord and will have to face some discouraging episodes there. There will be doors of opportunities that we think should automatically open to us, and when they don't open immediately, we often become discouraged and quit. But this story helps us to understand the importance of a commitment to keep on knocking because you are at the right place.

This word, "knocked," in Greek is *"Kru oh."* It means to keep on knocking. That is exactly what Peter did. I know this is true because he started knocking in verse 13, and when we jump down to verse 16, we read that Peter kept knocking. So let me encourage you to do what Peter did and keep on knocking, and God will send the help that you need. When the Lord has set you free, don't you dare turn back. Make up your mind to just tell the story about who set you free. The Lord is counting on you to be a good representative; don't let Him down.

CHAPTER 10

IT'S ALL WORKING TOGETHER FOR OUR GOOD

2 Corinthians 4:16–18
SERVICE

Introduction

Allow me to begin this chapter by sharing with you that I believe I stand on solid ground when I say that there have been times in our lives when we feel like quitting and throwing in the towel. Some of us may be experiencing a season like that right now. Often we try to keep these feelings bottled up inside for several reasons. In some instances, we think we are the only ones who may be going through what we are going through and feel like trouble is a sign of God's displeasure with our lives. In other instances, pride causes us to attempt to maintain our public images when we are literally hurting beyond description on the inside. We have a smile on our faces, but our hearts are filled with grief. Other times, we think that no one can help us through what we are dealing with.

These overwhelming feelings cause us to fail to recognize that Solomon said there is nothing new under the sun, which simply means that whatever we are facing, someone has already faced it before us. God saw them through it, and He will see us through it, if we just hold on and wait on Him.

73

I want to be as transparent as I possibly can and share with you how the Lord has helped me deal with my struggles and some of the lessons that I have learned from personal experiences. My greatest challenges in life and in my ministry have been faced and overcome when I became honest enough to admit them to God. That honesty led me to maintain my post in the area of ministry where He has positioned me, and then I was able to make a determination that I was not going to allow the devil to stop me from doing what I knew God had called me to do. I have learned how to trust the Lord either to resolve my issues or to give me the strength to deal with my issues and still remain productive in His kingdom. I am not going to give the devil the satisfaction of using trouble to break my relationship with the Lord. The Lord has given each of us the same kind of spiritual tenacity; all we have to do is use it.

I have discovered that satan does not always attack us overtly; in some instances, he does it subtlety. He causes us to simply sit quietly when praise is being raised or when we have an opportunity to verbally express our faith in God and our convictions about God. This happens because the devil knows what many of us don't realize. If we speak those words of victory and triumph with our mouths, we will also have a desire in our hearts to become people who are maturing in God's word, fulfilling our missions in the world, and magnifying God's name in worship. These are the last things that the devil wants us to be committed to doing. The enemy also knows that if we don't say it, we will not practice it, because the Bible says, "The power of death and life are in the tongue." We also need to learn the importance of verbally responding to the truth when it is preached from the Word of God. The Bible says that the redeemed of the Lord should "say so." Did you not know that if our excitement about the Word of God is void of enthusiasm, then our commitment to practice the principles of God's Word will also lack luster?

In this letter to the Christians in Corinth, Paul is striving to give them, and us, principles to hold on to despite hardships so we remain productive in the kingdom of God. He wanted those who lived during his lifetime, and those of us today, to live the kind of lives that are truly making a difference in the kingdom of God.

In verse 16, Paul says, "Therefore we do not lose heart. Even though our outward man is perishing, yet the inward man is being renewed day by day." What was Paul trying to get us to embrace as it pertains to this matter of service in the kingdom of God? I believe he wanted us to focus on the importance of:

I: Our Development

One of the most difficult lessons I have learned from the Lord is what I *desire from Him* is not always what He is trying to *develop in me*. Psalm 37:4 says, "Delight thyself in the Lord and He will give you the desires of your heart." The word "delight" as it is used in that passage means to pursue those things that please God. When we do this, our desires will also be things that please Him. Paul tells us "not to lose heart." In other words, don't give up! Why? Because the outward man is going to perish with or without more materialistic possessions. When we learn how to properly handle more of God's responsibilities, He will allow us to handle more of His resources. Many times, people ask me to pray for their businesses, their schooling, and their jobs, but I have to remind them of that all those things are perishable in nature. God is not interested in developing those things that are perishable in our lives, but He is trying to develop what is being renewed in our lives, like our faith in Him, our trust in Him, our work for Him, and our representation of Him. He allows us to go through what we go through because He is trying to make us better EVERY DAY—not weekly, monthly, or yearly, but daily. We are being renewed day by day!

In verse 17, he expands on the matter by sharing these helpful insights: "For our light affliction, which is but for a moment, is working for us a far more exceeding and eternal weight of glory." The more that we are developed by God, the better able we are to handle:

II: OUR DIFFICULTIES

Difficulties will come to hinder our spiritual progress. This verse is very comforting because Paul calls his troubles "light afflictions." One of the reasons we think our troubles are heavier than what they really are is because we are using the wrong measuring rod to determine their weight. If you really want to find out how much your trouble weighs, then compare them to God's Son coming into the world and being rejected by the very people that He created. Compare them to being crucified for guilty sinners when you never even knew what it meant to commit sin. Compare your trouble to being slapped and spat upon, your hands being pierced with nails, your feet being riveted, your side pierced, and being beaten by the very people you were about to die for. This is why Paul calls his troubles "light afflictions," because he compared them to Jesus. When we look at the trouble that Jesus went through for us, we will realize that He was sinless. Then consider what we are going through and that we are sinful; it forces us to ask ourselves if we still think that our trouble is heavy. We need to take a few moments to think about some of the things the Jesus went through and compare it to what we are going through, and then we will stop pouting and start shouting.

The assurance of this verse comes in knowing that all our problems are momentary. They may seem longer and heavier because we compare them to the wrong things. We compare our problems to what we feel and see around us. But Paul *compared his problems* to *the promise God* made for eternity after our trouble is all over. The manner in which we handle our problems will determine our promotion. The Lord is trying to elevate you to a new level in your relationship with Him and to a new level in your responsibilities for Him. My challenge to you is to stay faithful because you don't want to be out of position when the Lord starts passing out promotions. You need to know that God has more in store for us than what we can see right now.

Paul seems to put the spiritual icing on the Christian's cake in verse 18. He writes these encouraging words: "While we do not look at the things which are seen, but at the things which are not seen. For the things which are seen are temporary, but the things which are not seen are eternal." Paul seems to be giving us instructions for how to properly handle:

III: OUR DISTRACTIONS

What is blinding you, either partially or totally, from seeing Jesus and His will for your life? Whatever it is, walk away from it and move out of that demonic darkness into the luminous light of the Son of God.

Paul is attempting to make us aware of the fact that the only way we are going to have some real spiritual peace in our lives is for us to redirect our attention away from the temporary to the eternal. Too many of us have our focus and concentration in the wrong places. We are trying to do for ourselves what God has promised to do for us, and we have overlooked doing what He has commanded us to fulfill. Will you be honest and admit that many people are too consumed with how they are going to pay for and keep what they have? We are stressed about making a name for ourselves and making sure that we don't get left behind while others seem to be passing us by. Let me give you a few examples. We were stressed out about being approved for our materialistic possessions before we gained possession of them. Now that we have those things, we are stressed out about how we are going to keep up the payments, and we don't know what we are going to do if we lose it. While we are in a state of panic about these trivial things, we have completely overlooked what Jesus said in Matthew 6:33: "Seek ye first the kingdom of God and His righteousness and all of these things will be added to you."

Did you not know that since Jesus is able to handle the payment of sin for the whole world, there isn't anything that He wants us to have that He will not make sure we have the resources to be able to afford, when it is His will for us to have in the first place? What we buy for ourselves, we have to pay for. But the things He has for us in eternity have already been paid for. Everything we can see has time written on it. What He has for us has eternity stamped on it. The source of the power that keeps us motivated to go on even against the odds does not come from things we can see around us but from the invisible God who lives within us and sees what we are unable to see.

1 Corinthians 13:12 helps us to put this whole matter in its proper perspective. "Now we see through a glass darkly, but then face to face. Now we know in part, but then we shall know even as also we are known." In other words, "We'll understand it better by and by." But until then, keep trusting and allow the Lord to equip you to be used in His service at a level that will glorify Him and horrify the devil.

CHAPTER 11

WHY IN THE WORLD IS ALL THIS HAPPENING TO ME?

2 Corinthians 1:3–5
SERVICE

After more than thirty-six years of preaching the gospel of Jesus Christ and after more than thirty-two years of serving the Lord's people as a pastor, I know what it means to minister to people who are dealing with physical, emotional, and spiritual pain. In more instances than I can count or remember, I have sought to provide comfort and strength for God's people during some of the most difficult seasons in their lives. I have buried the dead of family members. I have counseled couples who were on the verge of divorce. I have prayed for people prior to them going under the surgeon's knife. I have even tried to help families who were dealing with a severe financial crisis. While I was seeking to minister to them, it caused me to place the personal pain and individual struggles that I may have been dealing with at the time in my own life on the back burner of my priority list. There have been many times early in my ministry when people have had more questions than I had answers; they had more problems than I had solutions. They had more burdens than I had relief, and they had more tears than I had comfort to share with them.

During some of those times, I was forced to rely on some of those old familiar phrases, we as "church folk" often resort to during times of tragedy. Phrases like, "God will never place more on you than you are able to bear." Or, "Just look to the hills from whence cometh your help, for all your help comes from the Lord." How could I ever not mention that time-tested favorite: "He may not come when you want Him to, but when He shows up, He will be right on time"? Now, I don't want you to misunderstand me, for I am by no means seeking to minimize the truth, importance, or power of these statements. These were statements that I was using simply because I had heard somebody else use them.

I have reached a point in my now where I have been able to discover that these words are much easier spoken by the person who is trying to offer the comfort than they are received and embraced by the person whose heart is filled with an enormous amount of pain. There are people all around us who are dealing with the dilemma of having no idea how they are going to get through the problems staring them in the face.

Allow me to take a moment to ask this question: Have you ever been at a point like this in your life? Well, if you have, you know exactly what I'm referring to. Now, allow me to digress for just a moment and ask you to consider the syntax and the grammatical arrangement that I used in a statement I made just a few moments ago. I said that there have been so many times "EARLY IN MY MINISTRY" that I was forced to rely on what I had heard other people say, because at that point I had not matured spiritually to the level where the Lord has me now in this season of my life.

> God has developed me, shaped me, and molded me, and now I am able to offer people something more than what I heard other people say.

Now I can truly minister to hurting people because of the things that God has allowed to take place in my own life. Allow me to share just a few of those things with you. I have experienced being married at the age of nineteen, trying to raise twins, and needing money for Similac, diapers, and baby food and then being laid off at my job. I've had cars repossessed and had to move from one house to another because I could not afford the rent payments. I've had people whom

I thought were my good friends lie to me, betray me, forsake me, and stab me in the back. I have experienced giving my all to the people of God only to have them misunderstand me and refuse to follow my God-ordained leadership. I have had years when I ran out of money before I ran out of month. I have had the struggle of trying to put two daughters through college while trying to get a third daughter out of high school.

In 2002, I had to bury my father, who was my best friend in the whole wide world. Then in 2008, the devil attacked my mind and my body, and I did not know if I was going to live or die. I was forced to live for more than two years with extreme emotional and mental pain. While I was going through that, the Lord called my mother home in January of 2009, and I had to preach her funeral and bury her, just as I had done for my father. All this is but a drop in the bucket of some of the things that the Lord has allowed me to endure.

But let me tell you the results of having to go through all those difficulties in my life. Now, when I give people words of comfort, now when I speak to people whose hearts are broken, my words are no longer clichés. They are testimonies that come from the depth of my own pain and deliverance. God has used every negative thing that I have gone through to get me to the point where He has me right now.

Now when I say, "The Lord will make a way," it is because He has made a way for me so many times. Now, when I say, "God will provide and make your enemies leave you alone," I can say that because I have watched Him put food on my table when I had no money in my pocket, and I have watched Him cause some of the very people who were laughing at me only a few short years ago to be amazed by all that He is doing in my life right now. But it took all of the negative things that occurred in my life to teach me how to be grateful for the positive things.

This is exactly what Paul is trying to get us to understand here in this first chapter of this book of 2 Corinthians. Allow me to share this truth with you. The bottom line to the whole matter is that we may not like what God is doing, we may not understand what God is doing, and we may not agree with what God is doing, but whatever God is doing, He has a purpose and a reason behind it that is bigger than each and every one of us.

Paul helps us understand that we need to have a desire to not only hold on during those seasons when we don't know why we are going through what it is we are going through, but also we need to know that God is trying to grow us, develop us, and mature us. And in order for this to happen, the first thing that we need to do is to have what I want to call:

I: A Disposition of Adoration

Follow me very closely here because I am about to bless you real good. In verses

4–11 of this chapter, Paul talks about the troubles that are inevitable in our lives. He teaches us how to place them in their proper perspective. But before he deals with the troubles in verse 4 that we are going to face, he begins by telling us in verse 3 what kind of attitude and disposition we should have even before the trouble rears its ugly head. He says, "Blessed be the God and Father of our Lord Jesus Christ, the Father of mercies and the God of all comfort."

> **I believe Paul is trying to get us to understand that there are some storms that we have just got to learn how to shout and praise our way through.**

When we learn how to develop a "shouting spirit" and a "rejoicing reputation," we can just bless God continuously, no matter what the devil may throw in our direction. The only way we will be able to do this is for us to focus more on God, because He is controlling our lives, than we focus on the devil, who is causing temporary havoc in our lives. I shared with you earlier in this chapter some of the temporary troubles that I have faced in my life, but I also need to tell you that I never allowed any of those situations to stop me from praising the Lord. People can say whatever they choose to say about me—some of it is true and some of it is not.

> **But nobody can honestly say that Roy Elton Brackins has ever allowed anything to stop him from publicly praising the Lord!**

You see I have found out a very important fact and that fact is, God's peace is permanent, but the devil's chaos is temporary. If Big Mama was here, she would
say it like this: "I'm so glad that trouble don't last always." Paul calls God the "Father of Jesus Christ." This helps us to understand that everything He allowed Jesus to go through. He brought Him out victorious on the other side of it. Then he calls Him the "Father of mercies." This enlightens us to the fact that He has already made provisions not only for the troubles other people bring into our lives, but also for the trouble that we bring on ourselves. Because in most instances, we have nobody to blame but ourselves for some of the poor choices that we have made. So aren't you glad to know that God continues to have mercy on you every time you go contrary to His Word?

He calls Him the "God of all comfort." The word "comfort" in Greek is *Par-ak-lay-sis*. It means to console and to be built up even while we are going through our troubles. God does not take away the trouble, but He teaches us how to walk with Him and how to depend on Him even while we are going through the trouble.

Then, in verse 4, Paul shares another important principle. He says, "Who comforts us in all our tribulation that we may be able to comfort those who are in any trouble with the comfort with which we ourselves are comforted by God." Are you still wondering, "Why is all of this happening to me?" Well, the Lord is trying to teach you some lessons about:

II: Development from Your Adversity

Paul gives us a clear and definitive answer here in verse 4, and he does it in a three-fold presentation. First, he gives us an *assurance*. Second, he gives us an *assignment*, and third, he gives us an *affirmation*.

Now, if I were preaching this sermon at Grace Tabernacle, I would ask for permission to make that block one more time. I'll drive a little slower on this trip. The **assurance** is found in the words, "Who comforts us in all of our tribulations." Not some of them, not just the ones that come into our lives from the hands of other people, not just the ones that last a few days, but the Lord gives us the assurance that He is right with us to comfort us in all our troubles! We would never be able to have an assurance of God's presence in our lives if He did not allow us to go through some seasons filled with tribulations. But then not only does the Lord give us His assurance, He also gives us an **assignment**. There it is! God takes us through our troubles so that we can help others get through their troubles, until they become mature enough to walk with Him all by themselves. Paul says, "That we may be able to comfort those who are in any trouble."

Let me show you what I'm talking about. I have four children, but none of them were born knowing how to walk. I had to walk with them when they were young so that I could teach them how to walk on their own once they got older. But while I was teaching them to walk, they all did a whole lot of falling down, but I was right there to lift them up and to tell them, "Go and try it again." And that is really the gist of our assignment from God. He allows us to go through some tribulations so that people who are not as strong as we are can look at us and ask, "Oh, is that how I'm supposed to handle the death of a loved one? Oh, is that how I'm supposed to handle a foreclosure? Oh, is that how I'm supposed to go through a job termination? Oh, that is how I'm supposed to handle a divorce. Oh, is that how I'm supposed to handle sickness in my body?" Now, let me pause parenthetically and ask an important question:

> **What kind of lessons are people who are weaker than you are learning from you about how to handle their tribulations?**

But then not only does the Lord give us His assurance and an assignment, He also gives us an *affirmation*. And the affirmation comes in the fact that Paul says at the end of the verse "with the comfort with which we ourselves are comforted of God." In other words, the more of God's comfort that we pass out, the more of His comfort we will receive. God uses our trouble to develop us into better humanistic comforters. We need to know that the Lord will never allow us to minister to the needs of other people without also having our own needs ministered to. These verses have made clear to us the importance of having a disposition of adoration. We have considered the development from adversity. But in verse 5, I see what I want to call:

III: The Divine Advantage

In other words, we are not suffering in vain, and we are not suffering without an eternal promise. Listen to what Paul says in verse 5: "For as the sufferings of Christ abound in us, so our consolation also abounds through Christ." The Twentieth Century New Testament translates verse 5 like this: "It is true that we have our full share of the sufferings of the Christ, but through the Christ we also have our full share of consolation." This is what I would call a "divine advantage." This verse is trying to get us to understand an important principle. If you ask an eighty-pound, ten-year-old child to lift a hundred-pound weight, it will be impossible for them. But if you ask a two-hundred-and-fifty-pound grown man to lift the same hundred pounds, he could do it with no problem.

Paul is trying to get us to understand that the only thing hindering us from carrying heavy sufferings is our spiritual immaturity. So God places us on an intensive workout regimen to build up our spiritual muscles. We can't get strong when all is going well in our lives. But when we are forced to go to the gym of grief, get on the treadmill of tribulations, bench-press our burdens, work on the abdominals of adversity, and climb the stair-master of stress, once we come out, we are stronger and ready to handle whatever the devil may send in our direction. If you were like I was when I was writing the chapter, you might have tears in your eyes now. Not tears of grief or sadness, but tears of praise and hope, because you can now better understand why all this either was or still is happening to you. It is because God is trying to make you more like Jesus. He is trying to give you a life filled with *passion for other people*. "Greater love has no man than this than for a man to lay down his life for his friends."

He is trying to give you a life that receives His *power for your purpose*. "As My Father hath sent Me, even so now I send you." And a life filled with *preparation for the pain*. "No man takes my life. I lay it down, and I have the power to pick it up again."

He died one Friday. He was buried, but early Sunday morning, He got up with all power in His hands! He is alive forever, and we shall also live with Him in eternity. Why is all this happening to you? Because God is using us to be a blessing and a source of spiritual strength for those who will face troublesome situations in their lives once He has delivered us.

CHAPTER 12

PICK UP YOUR PART OF THE LOAD!

Galatians 6:1–5
SERVICE

In Mark Chapter 2, we read a story about one man who is sick and cannot get to Jesus on his own power. But he had four friends who placed him on a palate, brought him to Jesus, and even climbed to the top of the house and tore the roof off so that their friend could be exposed to the presence of the Master. This helped me understand one of the many things that we as Christian believers need to be constantly reminded of: God did not save us and allow us to be a part of His Church simply for us to live isolated from each other.

He wants us to be connected to one another, intertwined with our fellow saints, and bonded together in spiritual unity. It was never part of God's plan for us to simply interact with one another for two hours once a week and then go back into our little individual worlds without any consistent interaction with the people who are supposed to have the same beliefs and values as we do and who worship and serve the same Christ as we do. There must be an unbreakable attachment of love between us that is stronger than our personal differences, ethnic diversity, economic distinctions, and educational characteristics. We are more than just people who gather in a building to fellowship with each other on a spiritual basis. We are a family. We are a royal priesthood. We are a part of the called, a chosen generation, a handpicked, fastidiously selected, and blood washed people of God. Did you not know that we have been redeemed by the precious blood of God's Son, Jesus Christ? Even when we are going through seasons of struggles, God has given us each other so that the strong can provide strength for those who are dealing with periods of weakness, and those who are weak can gain strength from those who are stronger. Many of us fail to realize that the best way for us to remain in a condition of being discouraged and distracted by the devil, is when we purposely isolate ourselves from the church and disconnect ourselves from our other brothers and sisters in Christ. The devil somehow causes us to believe that we are the only ones who are going through periods of difficulty in our lives. We have also been misled into believing that we have sinned beyond God's ability to forgive us and that there is no hope for us to be restored and be used again by God to His glory. The longer we stay away from the church and are disconnected from our brothers and sisters in Christ, the more difficult our problems will become.

After we have stayed away so long, the devil will tell us that we have been gone too long to go back now. But I have come to tell you that the only reason we having these thoughts and wrestling with these feelings is because of an ignorance of the Word of God. Now, don't be offended by that word "ignorance." This word simply means the lack of knowledge on a particular subject. And when we start thinking that we are the only ones who have made a mess of our lives, made poor choices, failed God more than one time, or found ourselves in a situation where everybody now knows about our sins, we struggle. I want you to know that there are people who sit in pews at church in front of you, behind you, and all around you, who will tell you that if you think that you are the only one who is dealing with these issues, that just means that we are ignorant of Romans 3:23. There we read, "All have sinned and come short of the glory of God." We are also ignorant of 1 John 1:9, where we read, "If we confess our sins, God is faithful and just to forgive us of our sins and to cleanse us from all unrighteousness." We are ignorant of Isaiah 1:18, where we read, "Come now, and let us reason together, says the Lord, though your sins are like scarlet, they shall be as white as snow; Though they are red like crimson, they shall be as wool."

And all I'm really trying to say is that we all have some issues and sins that we are dealing with. But the difference lies in that some of us choose to remain connected to our churches and make ourselves available for the service of the Lord despite our past mistakes. We have made a conscious decision to become attached to a ministry, and we are looking for opportunities to grow in the grace of God.

On the other hand, we have other people who simply wallow in their sins, remain isolated from the church, refuse to become connected, and allow the devil to use them as pawns in his demonic destructive deeds. The very fact that you have kept reading until this point means that you know you need to do either one of two things. The first may be to make up your mind right now that enough is enough.

> **You need to cry out to God and make a commitment to Him to seek His will, study His Word, and surrender to His plan, and not allow the devil to disconnect you from Him ever again.**

The second thing is to determine that you are not going to allow anything or anybody to stop you, hinder you, or slow you down from being effective and productive in the service of the Lord.

In Chapter 6 of the book of Galatians, Paul addresses the matter of the strong and the weak that are a part of the Church. He gives a detailed plan for how all of us should be working together so that we can live the kinds of lives that will make a difference in the kingdom of God—not just occupying space, but walking in our purpose; not just existing, but living that abundant life that Jesus came here for us to have; and not just sitting around waiting for the devil to attack us and defeat us with another ungodly temptation, but learning how to say no to him, so that we can say yes to Jesus Christ.

In verses 1 and 2, Paul tells us, "If a person is overtaken in a sin, those of us who are spiritually strong should restore that person with a spirit of gentleness, and we must also consider ourselves and be careful not to allow the same thing that took them down, to take us down." He also tells us to "bear one another's burdens and so fulfill the law of Christ." One of the best ways to offer quality, Spirit-filled service in the kingdom of God is by establishing a mindset of *a compassionate restoration*. Did you not know that the Bible is filled with what I want to call "*one another*" statements?

Well, if you did not know, let me share a few of them with you. We are told to "love one another," "forgive one another," "pray for one another," "support one another," "encourage one another," "edify one another," and "be kind and tender-hearted toward one another." And here in these verses, Paul is telling us about the need for the strong to "restore one another," and for us to "bear one another's burdens."

I have made a startling discovery, and the thing that I have discovered is that many people in the church are more interested in amputation than they are in restoration. We are more willing to get rid of people than help people heal and grow into becoming productive citizens in the kingdom of God. In verse 1, Paul is basically saying two things.

The person who has been overtaken in the fault is GUILTY, and they need somebody to offer them some GRACE!

He is not talking about a person who has purposefully chosen to live an ungodly lifestyle and then come running back to the church when they simply want to use us and want us to feel sorry for them. Paul is talking about that person who is really striving to be all that God would have for them to be but have allowed themselves to become caught up in a bad situation because of a decision that they made without seeking God's direction. Paul says we can reveal how strong and how spiritual we are, not by avoiding them or by getting rid of them, but by bearing them up during their time of weakness and expressing to them what the true love and mercy of Jesus Christ is all about. A person in a ditch needs a helping hand if he is going to get out of the ditch.

Then in verses 3 and 4, Paul issues a word of caution to all of us. In essence, he is saying that we had better be careful about evaluating ourselves. "For if a person thinks himself to be something, when he is nothing, he deceives himself; But let each one examine his own work, and then he will have rejoicing in himself alone and not in another." This helped me process that service in the kingdom of God also requires *personal evaluation.* Many of us are unable to do what God has assigned to our hands because we have become too preoccupied either with the things that other people are doing wrong or what they are not doing at all.

Did you not know that some people can only feel good about themselves when they tear somebody else down?

If we are going to evaluate ourselves properly, we need to use the correct standards. All those standards are housed in the Word of God. This is one of the reasons some people will run from Sunday school and Bible study, because they don't want to be told when they are wrong and what needs to be corrected in their lives. When we have this mindset, we wind up "deceiving ourselves." Now, its one thing for us to be able to convince other people with our lies, but it is a real sinful tragedy when we start to believe the lies that we know we are telling about ourselves. If we are going to evaluate ourselves according to the Lord's standards, we must use at least two principles.

Verse 3: Honesty: How transparent is your life, or how much stuff do you think you have to hide?

Verse 4: Helpfulness: How many other people are being blessed because of your faithfulness in the kingdom of God? We should be able to rejoice about the accomplishments of our church as a whole. Every person should be able to point to something specific and say, "MY church is a stronger and a better church because I do, this, that, or the other to help my church grow and become all that God would have her to be."

Finally, in verse 5, Paul says, "Each one shall bear his own burden." And this is where I have been trying to go. People who are weak in the body of Christ cannot use that as an excuse for a prolonged time. We need to accept some personal responsibility and realize that it's time for all of us to grow up and learn that we all have a part to play. You need to be serving and carrying your part of the load! We have been potty training some folks long enough; we have been changing diapers and burping some people for too long. We have been feeding some people from the bottle for too long! It is now time for you to bear your own burden.

We need to have *a compassionate restoration*, and we need to have some *personal evaluation*, but then finally we need some *dependable participation*.

Some people may think that there is a contradiction between verses 2 and 5. In verse 2, we are told to bear one another's burdens. But in verse 5, we are told that each man should bear his own burden. What we fail to realize is that the word "burden" in verse 2 means a load that is too heavy for one person to bear all by himself or herself. But the word "burden" in verse 5 is talking about a soldier's backpack. In other words, there will be some burdens that we all need some help with, but everybody should be able to carry their own individual backpacks. Jesus did this for us at Calvary. He carried a cross that was too heavy for us to carry all by ourselves. At least we can carry a tither's backpack. At least we can carry a Sunday school backpack. At least we should be able to carry one ministry's backpack. We should be able to carry an intercessory prayer warrior's backpack. Jesus carried what we could not carry so that we can carry what we can carry.

He carried our cross and died at Calvary, He was buried in a grave, and early Sunday morning, He got up with all power. Now we must serve Him by serving one another.

CHAPTER 13

MOTIVATING OUR MINDS FOR MINISTRY

1 Peter 1:13–16
SERVICE

One of the major things that we as believers in Jesus Christ must never lose sight of is that the devil will do whatever he can to prevent us from learning more about the Word of God. The apostle Paul recognized the need for us to have the Word of God housed in our hearts. So he wrote in 2 Timothy 2:15, "Study to show yourself approved unto God, a worker that does not need to be ashamed, rightly dividing the word of truth." Many of us fail to realize that in various instances, even satan recognizes that we are smarter than we think ourselves to be. And the reason I say this is because the devil has enough sense to know that when we learn more about Jesus Christ, and when we learn more about the Word of God, we will become better able to live the kind of lives that please our heavenly Father and that poses a threat to his demonic kingdom.

The devil will do everything in his power to cause us to become alienated from the study of God's Word in Bible study or the regular Sunday time that many churches have established. We will never mature spiritually when we allow ourselves to become distracted during the preaching of the gospel and start believing the lie that we are not cut out to become actively involved in ministry. The devil wants us to remain wide awake when we read other publications like *Ebony, People,*

Time, and *USA Today* and then cause our eyelids to feel like they weigh a hundred pounds before we can even get finished with one chapter of the Bible. Did you not know that the devil is aware of the fact that if you would get more of the Bible in you, you would really do some serious harm to him and to his kingdom? So he does all that he can to cause us to become sleepy when we read the Bible and to cause us to become disinterested and disconnected from our church, and we lose our joy as it relates to godly and spiritual things.

To the contrary, God has given us minds that are able to absorb His truths, develop a spiritual determination, and become resolved not to allow anything or anybody to prevent us from becoming all that we know in our hearts that He desires for us to be. When I think about this matter of how the devil wants to destroy our minds and cause us to become inactive and stationary in our relationship with the Lord, it reminds me of when I was a little boy growing up in Houston, Texas. The older people would always say, "An idle mind is the devil's workshop." And as I have grown older, I have found out that this is a true statement. Most of the people who grumble and complain about things in the church, about what the church should be doing and what the church is doing too much of, are the people who are doing little or nothing at all to help the church to reach the goals that God has placed before us.

Whenever we become inactive or slow down in our work in the church and our commitment to the church, we become prime candidates for the devil to use us as a tool of destruction and disruption. Did you not know that if we are going to motivate our minds for ministry, we must begin by *minimizing* the *mess* that fills our *minds?* We must *morally manage* the *manner* in which we use our *minds.* And we must *magnify* the *Master's mercy* in our *minds.*

In other words, we must be careful about what we allow our minds to become polluted with—such as all the gossip and idle talk that causes us to slow down in the work of the Lord as opposed to speeding up. Don't allow people to use your mind as a human garbage disposal for their stinking, sour, negative talk and unfounded rumors. We must also be careful what we allow our minds to lead us into doing. I have found out that before we commit an act, we always have to think about what we are preparing to do. This will help us to continue to magnify how merciful

God has been to us. His mercy has protected us and forgiven us, and even when we deserved punishment, He decided to give us His blessings. So, before we point the finger of accusation at somebody else, we need to check out our minds and start thinking about all of the evil, ungodly, immoral, and unholy things God has forgiven us for.

The Lord wants us to serve Him with pure, eager, and determined minds. Many times, we wonder why our minds seem to be so scattered and troubled, and the answer could very well be because we have our minds on everything else but the Lord. In Isaiah 26:3 we read, "You will keep him in perfect peace whose mind is stayed on You, because he trusts in You." When our minds are on the Word of God, the work of God, and the worship of God, He will keep us in perfect peace!

This is why Peter wrote in verse 13, "Therefore gird up the loins of your mind, be sober, and rest your hope fully upon the grace that is to be brought to you at the revelation of Jesus Christ." The Bible in Basic English translates verse 13 like this: "So make your minds ready, and keep on the watch, hoping with all your power for the grace which is to come to you at the revelation of Jesus Christ." This helped me to understand that we need:

I: A Mind Concentrated on the Promises of God

Peter tells us to "gird up the loins of our minds." When he uses the term "gird up," it helped his audience to understand a basic principle about their everyday surroundings. It is imperative for us to know that the people during that culture wore long, flowing garments, and before they would go into battle, they would gird up or tie all the lose ends of their garments so that they would not trip and fall while they were at war against the enemy. This is Peter's way of reminding us that we as believers in Jesus Christ are at war against the devil, and we need to have our minds girded so that we will not trip over any of the negative thoughts and words that he attempts to send into our mentality. The devil will use whatever he can to cause us to stumble and fall. He will use words like, "You are nothing. You are a failure; you will never make anything successful out of your life. You have no potential and no future." Words like, "You are not qualified to fill that position." Words like, "You really don't have anything to offer the kingdom of God." Words like, "You will always be a borrower and never a lender. You will always be the tail and never the head. You will always be on the bottom and never on the top."

But when our minds are girded up, we can speak back to the enemy and say, "I can do all things through Christ Jesus who strengthens me." We can say, "Greater is He who lives in me than he who lives in this world." We can say, "My mind is girded, and no weapon formed against me shall prosper." We can say, "When the wicked, even my enemy and my foes, came upon me to eat up my flesh, they stumbled and fell." We can say, "When my mother and my father forsake me, then the Lord will take me up."

But if our minds are not girded, we will trip and fall over every little thing that the devil puts in our pathway. Have you ever wondered why some people seem to keep making the same mistakes over and over again? They seem to do pretty good for about two or three months, and then they fall right back into that same old rut all over again? It is because they have not taken the time to gird their minds with the promises of God.

Peter says that we must be sober or keep watch. We must disciple ourselves so that we will learn how to deal with the difficulties that come our way. I have found out that the Christian life is not free from trouble, but the Christian life teaches us how to *evaluate* our troubles. It teaches us how to become *educated* from our trouble and then watch God *elevate* us above our trouble. That is why he says, "Rest your hope fully on the grace that is to be brought to you at the revelation of Jesus Christ." The term "rest your hope" is better translated as "fix your hope." Concentrate exclusively on Jesus Christ.

Did you not know that the only time we really get off track and get into trouble is when we stop concentrating on Jesus and start focusing on other stuff? This was not a theoretical suggestion from Peter; this was an experiential testimony from Peter. He knew firsthand what happened when he took his concentration off Jesus Christ. He was walking on the water, and when he started to look down at the waves, the Bible says "he started to sink." I hope you will agree with me when I say that when you take your eyes off Jesus Christ, you will also start to sink. But when your hope is fixed on Jesus, you are able to completely depend on Him to bring you through those difficult struggles and pitfalls that you have no idea how you got into in the first place. That is why he says "fix your hope." Hope always deals with the future. We must learn to believe that what God has planned for our future is much greater than what we are going through right now. And we will experience it all at the revelation or the coming of Jesus Christ because when He returns, all the heartache and pain, all the difficulty, all the burdens, all the despair and depression that we have gone through will be brought to an end.

In verse 14, Peter wrote these words: "As obedient children, not conforming yourselves to the former lusts, as in your ignorance." We need:

II: A Mind Consecrated by the Principles of God

After our minds are concentrated on the promises of God, we need to move to the next level of allowing the Holy Spirit to consecrate our minds on the principles of God. Allow me to pause parenthetically and ask some questions. What principles are really governing your life? Do you obey God only when it's convenient? Do you have a Sunday lifestyle from 7:45 a.m. to about 6:00 p.m. and then something diametrically opposite from Sunday night through Saturday night? Peter says we should be acting like obedient children. *And I already know that this next statement is going to offend some people, but you will get over it.* When we fail to obey what God has commanded us to do in His word, all we are really doing is showing our ignorance about the Bible. It is right here in the text. He says we should not be conforming to our old ways, digressing into our old habits, and returning to our old lusts because all that shows is how ignorant we are of the great things that God has delivered us from. What is it that you used to do before you surrendered your life to Jesus that you don't do at all now that you are a Christian? Many of us have not stopped our sins; we have just slowed down and learned how to camouflage them better.

God is looking for obedient children. I believe I speak for every responsible, godly parent who has ever lived when I say nobody enjoys being around what my parents called hardheaded children. These are children who are determined to do things their own way; they are children who refuse to listen to and obey their parents. If we as sinful and earthly parents don't want our children disobeying us, what makes us think that it is all right for us to disobey our heavenly Father? He has done 10 bazillion times more for us than we have done for our children.

Peter uses a very interesting term in this verse. He writes, "Not conforming to your old lusts." This means to digress into the very things that God has delivered us from. We often tell our children, "You are too big to be acting like that." The Lord is speaking to us through Peter, and He is saying that it's time for us to grow up as believers. It's time for us to show some signs of spiritual maturity. The devil should not be defeating you as much now that you are a ten-year-old Christian as he was when you were a six-month-old Christian.

We must not succumb to the conforming temptations of the devil. The devil wants us to act like him, dress like him, talk like him, and even retaliate like him. But our standards should be *higher*, our lifestyles should be *holier*, and our conduct ought to be *heavenly*. The only way that we will be able to do this on a consistent basis is to yield to the Holy Spirit and allow Him to keep our minds on the principles of God. We also need to know that the principles of God will not just pop into our minds. We must study the Word of God, and we must make the time to hear the preaching and teaching of the Word of God. The Bible tells us in 2 Corinthians 10:4 that "the weapons of our warfare are not carnal but mighty in God for pulling down strongholds." This helped me realize that the only way we can successfully fight and defeat the devil is not with a gun, knife, or fist. The only way we can defeat him is with the Word of God.

In Verses 15 and 16, Peter writes, "But as He who called you is holy, you also be holy in all your conduct, because it is written, 'Be holy, for I am holy.'" This helped me realize that we also need:

III: A Mind Committed to the Purity of God.

We live during a time when we hear a lot of talk and preaching about increase, prosperity, overflow, abundance, favor, opening flood gates, and next-level living. But we don't hear much preaching about holiness and godly living. Here in this text, Peter is informing us that we should be living like the one who has called us out of the darkness and into the marvelous light. I cannot for the life of me understand why we would claim we are called and saved by God yet act like the world, dress like the world, and behave like the world. God is calling for holiness. And even if we do stumble and sin, we should be ashamed of our sins. You had better check yourself when you become comfortable living the kind of lifestyle that the Bible says is sin in the sight of God. It may not be popular, but the truth of the matter is Jesus did not die for us to have equal rights. Jesus did not die for us to have alternative lifestyles. Jesus did not die for us to have freedom of choice. Jesus did not die for us to fit in with the crowd. Jesus did not die for us to have civil rights.

Jesus died for us to be delivered from our sins. He died for us to be free from our old lifestyles, and He died for us to be raised to a new standard of Godly living. I thank God that His death is not the end of the story, for He got up with all power in His hands. Now it's up to us to keep our minds focused on Him and get busy serving Him!

CHAPTER 14

IS HIS SUFFERING WORTHY OF OUR SERVICE?

I Peter 3:18–22
SERVICE

I have a tremendous amount of difficulty attempting to explain how much it saddens my heart when I see the one-sided relationships that many Christians have with Jesus Christ. I talk with some people regularly who claim that they are a part of the Body of Christ, and I hear the same thing from them over and over again. They all make a statement like this: "Pastor Brackins, I know that the Lord has been good to me." But I never hear them talking about anything that they are doing for the Lord. We have digressed so far away from what real Christianity is all about, and we only want Him to be a God who gives to us and never expects anything in return. We want Him to be a God who answers to our every beck and call but we will only respond to Him when it's convenient for us. We want Him to be a God who heals us, delivers us, provides for us, and protects us, but on the other side of the coin, many of us cannot even remember the last time we truly sacrificed something for the Lord.

There is a difference between giving to God and sacrificing for the Lord. A sacrifice is something that is near and dear to our hearts and is something that we would love to keep for ourselves. This is why Jesus is called the "perfect sacrifice." He was not God's second choice. He was the very best that God had, because when God gave us Jesus, He literally gave us Himself. But on the other side of the equation, we often operate in our relationship with the Lord like a malfunctioned sponge. We soak up all His blessings and squeeze out very little to nothing back to Him in return. I truly believe the testimony of any person who claims how God has opened doors for them, made ways for them, healed their bodies, brought their families back together, and gave them stable employment, yet they are inactive, untimely, robbers of the tithe, mean in their dispositions, and stagnant in their spiritual growth.

The testimony of such people leaves many unanswered questions. Why are you not doing more for Him? Many of us know what God has done for us, but the question before us today is what we have done and what we are presently doing for Him. I believe that one of the main problems with this kind of attitude lies in the fact that we are more focused on what God has in His hand rather than pursuing the love that He has for us in His heart. We must redirect our

focus away from just thinking that He is a God of cars, cash, clothes, cribs, and companions and return to the fact that He is a God of Calvary. All that we enjoy now in this world in which we live, and everything that has been promised and provided for us in heaven, is inextricably intertwined with the suffering, death, burial, and resurrection of Jesus Christ. So I think I need to pause right here and ask the question again, since we know that He went through excruciating suffering for us: Are we willing to offer excellent service for Him? Many of us can point to the things that God has done for us. But can we also identify some things that we have committed ourselves to, so that He will be glorified through us.

The people that Peter was writing to were not concerned about trivial matters like what somebody had on or did not have on. They were not worried about whose skirt was too short and whose blouse was too tight. They were not focused on who had on tennis shoes and who had on dress shoes. They were not concerned with who was going to lead the ministry and who was going to follow. All they wanted to know was what the Lord was expecting from them so that they could prepare themselves to fulfill His assignments for their lives.

Peter reminds them and us as well in verse 18 of the fact that "Christ also suffered once for sins, the just for the unjust, that He might bring us to God, being put to death in the flesh but made alive by the Spirit." When we consider what greater level of service we can offer God to express our appreciation to Him for His suffering for us, this verse helps us to recognize that a good place to start would be by striving to improve our:

I: Relationship with the Lord

In the earlier verses of this chapter, we have been told to submit to one another and be ready to suffer, even when we are doing what is right. This was Peter's way of informing us that we really have no right to complain about our suffering because we are all sinners. Jesus is perfect, sinless, and free from any flaws, and He suffered for all of us.

Notice if you will what this verse says. Jesus Christ has suffered once for our sins, He was a just, holy, upright, and righteous man who suffered for ungodly, unholy, immoral, evil, gross, and arrogant people like you and me. And Peter tells us why He did it all. The middle part of the verse says "that He might bring us to God." The phrase "bring us to God" means that Jesus wanted to introduce and present us before His Father. This gave me so much encouragement just to know that He is proud of us despite our sinful condition that He wanted His Father to meet us, and many of us have never introduced our holy heavenly Father to another evil sinner similar to ourselves before we were saved. Have you taken any time to consider that Jesus wants each of us to have a relationship with His Father despite what He knows about us?

Let me show you what I'm trying to get you to understand. There are many people who will quickly tell others things like, "No, you better stay away from him." "Man, you don't want to have anything to do with her." "Girl, don't you start hanging around with them; they are nothing but trouble and bad news." But Jesus has never told His Father, "Daddy, you don't want to meet him and let him into heaven because he has been to jail." "Daddy, you don't want her singing your praise; she had children out of wedlock." "Daddy, you don't want to call him to preach your word; he used to be a crack addict and an alcoholic."

Jesus has cleaned us up, washed us in His blood, and saved us, and one of these days, we will be presented to His Father as the bride of Christ. So with all this in mind, I need to ask how we can not serve a God who has done all of this for us and who desires to have a relationship with us despite all the dirt that He knows on us. This verse tells us that Jesus was put to death in His flesh, and He was also made alive by the Spirit. Jesus not only died for us, but He also now lives within us. He does not simply come to visit us on a sporadic basis; He lives within us all day, every day. And the only reason He does this is because He is striving to improve our relationship with Him, and His hopes are that we will come to know Him better so that we will serve Him better.

We see even more good news for us to consider here in verses 19 and 20. Peter says, "By whom also He went and preached to the spirits in prison, who formerly were disobedient, when once the Divine longsuf-fering waited in the days of Noah, while the ark was being prepared, in which a few, that is, eight souls were saved through water." This lets me know that:

II: We've Been Rescued by the Lord

Are you willing to testify that God has bailed you out of some situations and rescued you from things that you had no idea how you were going to get out of? Allow me to take a few moments to clear up a misinterpreta-tion of scripture that I have been guilty of for many years. I used to say that after Jesus died, "He went down into hell and preached a revival to the spirits." This scripture was the basis for my statement. But I had to confess and ask my congregation to forgive me because I was misrepre-senting the truth of this verse. This verse is not intended to imply that Jesus went to hell and preached after His death. Catholics use this verse as a basis for their belief in purgatory. They say that Jesus allowed all of the evil people to remain alive until His death, and then He went down to hell and set them free. The only reason many of us misinterpret the meaning of this verse is because we did not connect verse 19 with verse 20. We are told in verse 20 that only eight souls were saved from the flood. Peter is trying to get us to understand that Jesus Christ preached to unbelieving men through the prophet Noah, and He gave them 120 years to repent. They were literally in the prison of sin, because Genesis 6:5 says, "Then the Lord saw that the wickedness of man was great in the earth, and that every intent of the thoughts of his heart was only evil continuously."

Peter was trying to get us to understand that God is still willing to rescue us from our sins, but He always does it through the preaching of one of His representatives. God will wait on us, but if you are not saved, you are taking a heaven and hell chance by not accepting Him today because you never know when your time to be rescued will be over. The reason he mentions that only eight souls were saved is because there are always more people who reject Jesus than there are who accept Jesus. But I do want you to know that the text says that Noah and his family were saved through water. In other words, the same thing that destroyed the unbelievers was used by God to save the believers.

Now, you may want to know how could water destroy one crowd and save another crowd. How can pain destroy one crowd and save another crowd? How can divorce destroy one crowd and save another crowd? How can a job layoff destroy one crowd and save another crowd? Well, I've kept you in suspense long enough. The evil people allowed the water to overcome them, so they were destroyed, while the godly people got in the ark and floated on top of what others allowed to overcome them. All I'm trying to get you to understand is that trouble will come, but you don't have to allow it to destroy you. Just get in the ark of God's vessels called salvation and the Church, and you have the ability to float right on top of your troubles until the storm passes over! This is why we should be offering God more of our service because He has rescued us from the very things that should have killed us and caused us to lose our minds.

In verses 21 and 22, Peter says, "There is also an antitype which now saves us—baptism (not the removal of filth from the flesh, but the answer of a good conscience toward God), through the resurrection of Jesus Christ, who has gone into heaven and is at the right hand of God, angels and authorities and powers having been made subject to Him." I've tried to tell you that we should be willing to give God more of our service because He wants to have a closer *relationship* with us. He also has loved us enough to *rescue* us. But finally, these verses help me understand that the Lord has:

III: Redeemed Us

He tells us that the flood was only an antitype in the flesh for what Jesus has done for us in our souls. And this word, antitype, means an Old Testament example of a New Testament reality. Peter makes the fact clear that when he mentions baptism and that he is not talking about going into a baptismal pool, because that may wash our bodies from filth, but it cannot wash our souls from sin.

Now let me try to tie all this together so that we can have clarity in our minds. I believe the reason Peter mentions baptism, the flood, and salvation is because they all have at least three things in common. First of all, we must *believe*. People should only be baptized because they **believe** in Jesus Christ. The only way to escape the flood was to **believe** in the preaching of Noah, and the only way you can be saved is to **believe** that Jesus has died for your sins.

Secondly, we must *repent* while we still have time. Baptism is an outward sign to the world that we have **repented** from our sins in our hearts. The people during the days of Noah were destroyed because they refused to **repent,** and they kept right on with their evil practices until the days of the flood. We cannot truly follow Jesus unless we have **repented** from our old lifestyles and decided to make Him our choice.

Then there must be a coming out of the old and an *entering* in of the new. Baptism is a sign to the world that we are coming out of the old lifestyle and are *entering* into the water to become identified with Jesus Christ. The only reason Noah and his family were saved is because they had enough faith to come from the outside and to *enter* the inside of the ark. And Paul says, "If any man be IN Christ he is a new creature." So when we come to Jesus, we also need to *enter* His church and become a part of a family. That is when we will learn how to have a good conscience toward God. And just in case we should happen to stumble and fall on our Christian journey, we don't have to quit and give up because Jesus is now seated at the right hand of God. This verse says that angels, authorities, and powers have been made subject unto Him.

The only reason you were able to sleep without somebody taking your life last night is because Jesus told an angel to set up a guard outside of your home, and because He has so much power, they had to obey

His command. The only reason the authorities did not give you life in prison when you should have been found guilty is because Jesus made the authorities drop the charges after He had paid your bail. The only reason you have that job and the only reason your enemy has not been able to take you out is because Jesus has power to make folk hire you who don't even like you, and He has enough power to make your enemies leave you alone. I don't know about you, but that is enough for me to give God more of my service.

He has a Desire to have a relationship with us.

He has rescued us.

He has redeemed us.

Stewardship
of the
Wealth of the Lord

CHAPTER 15

WHAT ARE GOD'S BLESSINGS WORTH TO YOU?

Psalm 116:12
STEWARDSHIP

As we embark on establishing a new level of faith, trust, and confidence in God with our financial resources, I believe the first thing that we need to do is assess our relationship and commitment to the Lord. During the month of January, many of us make what are called "New Year's Resolutions," but I believe what we really need to do is reflect on the things that God has already brought us through, the blessings that God has sent our way, and the storms that God has not allowed to completely wipe us out. We are here and alive because of God's amazing grace. He has protected us, provided for us, and when we were guilty, He has pardoned us through the blood of His Son, Jesus Christ.

We need to take a moment and ask ourselves if we have really been fair with God when it comes to the amount of our time, talent, and treasure that we have given to Him. We have placed His work on hold and failed to fulfill our financial responsibilities to Him and to His church because we were striving to pay other people who don't even know us by our names. To them, we are nothing more than an account number, an address, or a Social Security number. We struggle to keep our commitments to people and companies who only view us as nothing more than a regular customer that they can make money from.

But Jesus tells us that our heavenly Father knows the number of the strands of hair on our heads. When it comes to this matter of us being more committed and liberal to the Lord with our finances, there is one question that often comes to my mind and helps to put this whole matter in its proper perspective. That question is if you were God, what would you charge for eyes, minds, hearing, smell, and taste? What would you charge for the ability to walk, 206 bones in the human body, seven quarts of blood in your veins, and activity in your limbs? What would you charge for salvation, sanctification, and spiritual liberation? What would you charge for traveling grace to and from work, and we use that grace to work on jobs that keep us from being present at His house? What would you charge for arriving mercy, even when we are going to places that we know we have know business going there?

Well, I don't know what you would charge, but I can almost guarantee you that it would be more than a dime from every dollar. I have discovered that when it comes to our finances, many of us choose the easy way out and always look for excuses not to be more faithful to God with our money. Have you not taken the time to consider that everything that we have comes from God, so if we are going to give anybody our money, we should first of all give to the one who has blessed us with everything that we have? We don't give to God because we think that He needs what we have, we give to God because He deserves everything that we have. I would not serve a God who was broke and needed what I had. I serve a God who is rich and who has an abundant supply for all of His children.

Allow me to ask you a few questions. How much is God's joy worth to you? How much is His peace worth to you? How much is His Word worth to you? How much is His mercy worth to you? How much is His grace, His forgiveness, His steadfastness, His protection, His guidance, His favor, His healing, and His longsuffering worth to you? In what ways do you strive to let God know how much you appreciate Him by sharing with Him more than what He requires? I am again striving to emphasize the fact keep that the tithe is just the starting point of our giving. When we tithe, all we have done is given God what His word requires from us. Nobody wants to be in a relationship where a person gives to you only because he or she is required to give.

The question before us now is in what way do you let God know how much you love Him with your money? There are many women who would quickly terminate a relationship if they found out that the man they are married to or in a serious relationship with is spending more money on another woman, or other women, than he is spending on them. Whenever I am teaching stewardship principles, I take the time to ask the following questions. Do you love the Lord more than you love your car, home, or bills? Then I wait for the answer; there is always a unanimous yes! Then I ask, "How is your love for the Lord reflected in how much money you give for your mortgage, car note, and your bills? Well, how could you survive if God terminated His salvation of us because we choose to spend more money on things that satisfy us than we do on things that will enhance the kingdom of God? The Lord wants us to recognize that we will never have all that He desires for us to have, until we learn how to give Him our first fruits and our best gifts."

I was reading the books of Leviticus and Deuteronomy in my morning devotional reading, and there was one thing that the Lord said to His people over and over again concerning their responsibility to give to Him. He told them that they were not to offer Him any blemished animals as sacrifices. In other words, God would not accept from them those things that they did not even want for themselves. He wanted the best fruit, the best animals, the best gold, the best silver, the best grain, the best produce, and the best offerings. God has been good to us and He deserves nothing less than our vey best. Often I hear people say that the reason that they don't give to the church is because they are not about to give and help somebody else live an abundant life. Well, I wonder why we give to Wal-Mart, Dillard's, McDonald's, Papadeaux, Red Lobster, Macy's, Neiman's, Ross, and T. J. Maxx.

Do you actually think any of those people who own those companies are suffering in their lifestyles? Let me tell you why we give them our hard-earned money. It is because they meet a temporary need.

> **But when we give to the God, we give to Him because He meets an eternal need.**

113

We have to keep paying those other institutions, and if we fail to pay them, they will not allow us to use any of their merchandise. I want to take a few moments to remind us that God has kept giving us His air to breathe, His eyes to see with, His legs to walk on, His food to eat, His body to live in, and His mind to think with, even though many people have robbed Him of the tithe and failed to give to Him generously.

I believe this is the reason the psalmist lifts this question before us in this text: "What shall I render to the Lord for all His benefits toward me?" As we approach this matter of stewardship, I want to recommend that we get started with:

I: The Consideration of Our Possessions

I am about to make a statement that most of us have heard many times in church, and we love to hear it because it gives us a great amount of comfort. That statement is that you can't give what you don't have. But what most of us fail to realize is that the reason we find comfort in this statement is because we have spent our money in so many other places and doing so many other things that now we really don't have much of anything left to give to the Lord. What we need to realize is that this question is not an after-he-has-paid-his-bills question. This is a before-he-has-spent-one-dime-of-his-resources question. In other words, when he looked at everything that the Lord had given to him and before he gives anything to anybody else, he wanted to give the most to the One who deserved the most. So he asked, "What shall I render?" The psalmist is pondering, "What shall I give?" God has given me all this, and I dare not give it away to other people and then give Him the crumbs of what I have left.

Let me paint this picture in a contemporary fashion. He does not cash his check first and pay a few bills and ask this question. Instead, the question is raised even before he arrives at the check-cashing agency. This passage helped my wife and I make a major transition in our mind-set concerning our giving in 2002. We made a commitment to the Lord that we would never live in a house with a mortgage or drive a car or have any bill that is more than what we give to the Lord on a regular monthly basis. You may not agree with me, but we cannot honestly say that we love God more than our home, car, or other possessions, and we refuse to give them more of our money than we give to God. So the psalmist asks, "What shall I render?"

But then not only does this text teach us about the need to *consider our possessions*. The verse also includes the words "to the Lord." This part of the verse helped me to understand that we all need a:

II: Consciousness of Our Provider

The psalmist had no problem with giving lavishly to the Lord because he knew who God truly was in His life. We will never be able to give to God at an accelerated level until we come to recognize that it is by His grace that we are still alive and have the ability to get what we have. Deuteronomy 8:18a says, "And you shall remember the Lord your God, for it is He who gives you power to get wealth." In other words, whatever money we make from our jobs, it is because God gives us the minds to think with on our jobs and the strength to work with on our jobs. Many times people will say, "This is my money and I worked hard for this money." Well, I need to ask the question, how much money could you earn without God's hands, feet, eyes, fingers, toes, and mind?" What we give to God can just be considered as rental payments for using His tools to make a living.

Let me show you what I'm talking about. We had a bulb to go out in our church sanctuary, and it was too high for us to reach with a ladder so we had to rent a lift from a company that owned one so that we could replace the bulb. We did not own the lift; we just paid to use the lift. Well, since we don't own any legs, feet, minds, blood, oxygen, or any eyes to work with, the least we can do is to pay God some rent for using His tools called a body. For without His body, we would not have the ability to make a living for ourselves.

But then finally, the verse ends by saying, "for all of His benefits toward me." God has given us all our possessions, and He has been our constant provider. Now let me say a word about my:

III: Confidence in His Perpetuation

Notice what the verse informs us of: "for all of His benefits toward me." Not just one benefit, but benefits! They are perpetual. They keep on coming.

He tells us about at least three things that he recognizes about God's goodness in His life from this part of the verse. First of all, he recognizes that God's blessings have been *plenteous*. We know this is true because he says "for all." This "all" that he refers to includes, all His keeping, all His sustaining, all His forgiveness, all His mercy, and all His grace. But then not only were the blessings *plenteous,* they were also *protective*. That is the reason he calls them benefits. And we all know that benefits kick in whenever we have a time of sickness and/or unemployment. This was the psalmist's way of saying that God took care of him even when he could not take care of himself. God protected him even when he was fired and laid off. And then finally, he tells us about that God's goodness was *personal*. He says, "all of His benefits toward me." God knows how to bless you with just what you really need. But there is one thing that the psalmist could not add to his reason for giving to God because Jesus had not yet come in the flesh. We all know that one Friday at a hill called Calvary, He died for us and was buried for us, but early one Sunday morning, He got up with all power in His hands.

What shall I render unto the Lord? All that I have!

CHAPTER 16

IT'S AN INSIDE JOB

Malachi 3:8–10
STEWARDSHIP

This chapter is the actual sermon manuscript that I preached from in July of 2011. Let's get in a Sunday morning mindset and hear the Lord speak to our hearts privately as He spoke to the hearts of His people publically on the Lord's Day.

If you will, allow me to begin this sermonic presentation with a sincere, heartfelt, and genuine apology. I feel like I need to ask for your forgiveness for my failure to be clear in teaching and explaining the truth of the tithing principles and practices. We are striving to become a body of believers and a church family that operates in honest financial integrity, with members who are faithful and obedient to the Lord in honoring Him with the first fruits of all our financial resources. So, I believe that I owe some, if not many of you, an apology for not completely and clearly explaining what the tithe is and what our responsibilities as Christians are in presenting to the Lord what rightfully belongs to Him.

The reason that I feel that I owe you an apology and that I have a need to be more clear and understandable in teaching and preaching these principles is based on the responses, both verbally and written, that I have received from many of you as it relates to your reasons for not being a better steward with the money that the Lord has placed in your hands. Let me share a few of them with you:

- "Pastor Brackins, I am not working now, and I don't have any money to give."
- "Pastor Brackins, I am on unemployment, and I only get paid once a month."
- "Pastor Brackins, my hours have been cut back on my job, and I don't make as much as I used to make."
- "Pastor Brackins, after I pay all my bills, I just don't have anything left to give to the Lord."
- "Pastor Brackins, as soon as I get caught up with some of my past-due bills, I do plan to start tithing again."

After receiving these and other responses, I think I need to take some time to meticulously address each of these statements, with the hope that every one of us will leave here today with a clear understanding as to what the Lord not only expects from us but also requires from us. The sad reality of the matter is that most of the robbery that takes place at the church is not on the parking lot from cars being broken into. Most of it is AN INSIDE JOB.

Let me set the stage for the presentation of this sermon. I would not feel comfortable at the bank tomorrow if I knew that the person in front of me or behind me in line was a robber. I would not feel comfortable at the grocery store if I knew that the person in front of me or behind me was a robber. I would not feel comfortable at the gas station if I knew that the driver of the car at the pump beside me was a robber. I would not feel comfortable at the restaurant if I knew that the person sitting at the table beside me was a robber. Would you? Well, I cannot help but wonder how it is that we have become so comfortable when at least four hundred people come to church during one of our four weekly worship experiences and more than two hundred of them are robbers. May I tell you why we are so comfortable? It is because we are not the ones who are being robbed! The people who rob us at the bank, gas station, restaurant and grocery store, are people who do not know us, and we have not made any sacrifices for them. But when Christians rob the Lord of the tithe, we are not robbing a stranger. We are robbing the man who gives us the very air that we breathe, the blood in our veins, and the strength in our bodies, and the man who allowed

His only son, Jesus Christ, to die for our sins and raised Him for our salvation. Then we thank Him by highjacking Him week after week with our failure to give Him something as small as a dime from every dollar. We pay people who don't even know us and rob the One who created us. I tell you, "It's an inside job."

Allow me to digress for a few moments and address the concerns that I lifted in the opening of this sermon. First of all, tithing *is not* giving. The tithe is a debt that we owe to the Lord. The Lord has warned me to deal with this matter of robbery, just as I would not allow someone from the outside to rob the finance room each week and serve in a ministry leadership position. The Lord has said to me that He will not tolerate leaders and people who claim that they are His children to live guilt-free from wearing the label of **inside robbery**. Jesus said, "Where your treasure is, there will your heart be also." Our hearts as the people of God cannot possibly be in our ministries if we don't have at least 10 percent of our treasure in the church. My concern is only with our tithing, or the lack thereof. Let me explain it in detail.

Tithing is 10 percent of all the money that we receive, no matter where it comes from work money, unemployment money, insurance money, birthday present money, income tax return money, dead-aunt-who-left–you-five-thousand-dollars in her will money, and baby daddy/ child support money. It even includes the money you win when you play the lotto or the scratch-off. We owe God the first 10 percent of everything that He allows to come into our possession.

Secondly, if you have NO INCOME, you do not owe God anything. Tithing *is not* a set amount; it is *a percentage*. But no source of income also means that you have some explaining to do as to how your car note, rent, mortgage, light bill, clothes, and vacations are being paid for with no money. Just because it is not a regular job does not exclude us from giving to God the first 10 percent of whatever He has blessed us with no matter where it has come from. And those of us who need a financial miracle from God need to know that it will never come as long as we are guilty of robbing Him. If your hours have been cut back on your job, then the tithe is just 10 percent of whatever the weekly or monthly gross amount of your paycheck is. Remember, **we are not** talking about **giving**, but about *tithing*.

Then, for those of you who say, "After I pay all of my bills, I don't have anything left." What you fail to recognize is that God should be paid *first*. There is no such thing as we cannot AFFORD to tithe. Dr. Wyatt Walker has said, "Any Christian who does who does not tithe is a robber, and any Christian who says they cannot tithe is a liar, because God will never tell us to do something without also giving us the ability to fulfill His command." Maybe we cannot afford our homes, cars, clothes, and jewelry, but Tithing is the first thing that God requires from us. We must get to a point where we trust God to do what He said He would do, which is to meet and to supply all of our needs. When we fail to tithe, it is not a financial matter; it is a trust matter. If we truly trusted the Lord, we would obey Him consistently and with commitment.

If you have ever tithed, I want you to take a moment to ask yourself some questions. How has tithing caused your financial condition to get worse? How has robbing God improved your financial portfolio? Most of us spend more for a tank of gas each week than we give to the Lord. Sixty dollars each week for a tank of gas times twenty-six weeks equals one thousand, five hundred and sixty dollars. And many of us have given less than five hundred dollars in twenty-six weeks. How many times has Mr. Exxon answered your prayers? How many times has Mr. Shell healed your body? How many times has Mr. Texaco kept you clothed and in your right mind? I also need to say that we cannot buy things for the church like paper, pens, supplies, gifts, and food and say that is our tithe. All those purchases fall under the category of our giving.

The tithe is holy unto the Lord, and it must be presented to Him first! If we would all tithe, nobody would have to buy anything extra, because we would be able to meet those needs from the resources that would already be in the house of the Lord that this text speaks about.

Then when we say, "As soon as I get caught up on my bills, I will start tithing." What we are saying is, "God, as soon as I finish using Your money to pay all of these other nasty, mean, low-down, high-interest, telephone-harassing creditors, then I will pay You, who has been nothing but loving, kind, faithful, sacrificial, and forgiving to me." What we are saying is, "Lord, I fear them, more than I love You." Because we give to the one that we love, reverence, respect, and feel like we owe the most to. We need to take a moment to seriously and soberly ask ourselves a question. "How can we honestly say that we trust God with our souls, and we trust Him to provide for us throughout all of eternity, ten billion times ten billion years and more, and yet we don't trust Him with a tithe, because we are worried about a light bill, car note, and rent that is due next week?

I also need to tell us that one of the best and easiest ways to keep up with your tithing and never get behind again is to pay the Lord the first 10% as soon as we get any money from anywhere. Make it a practice to keep some Church envelopes with you.

I also need to say this. I am asking that a person who is not committed to trusting the Lord with your tithe on a consistent basis, not give anything else again in my love offering. **(I live on the love offering. If they give nothing, that is what I have to work with, but God has never allowed that to happen in twenty-five years.)**

Back to the Sermon

I have faith enough to believe that God will touch the hearts of other people to increase their giving so that the needs for my family and me will be met. I don't want to be guilty of receiving robbed money.

Now, let's look at the text:

Will a man rob God? Only you can answer that. Does this sermon bother you; does it trouble you enough to change so that the next time I preach about it, I will not be talking about you? God says we are guilty of robbing Him of the tithe and the offering. I will preach about the offering next time. Because of our actions, we are cursed with a curse. As soon as you try to get ahead, something else happens to your finances. The Lord is saying you have locked yourself into a confined area because of your stubbornness and determination to do things your way and ignoring His command.

This leads me to my first point. Look at verse 10. "Bring ye all the tithe."

I: Continuous Presentation

This means that we must keep on bringing; it must not be a one-time act. It must not be limited only to the times we feel like we are not having any financial challenges.

II: Complete Portion

"Into the Storehouse." Don't present 5, 6, 7, or 8 percent. If you do, you are still guilty of robbery. If I go to the bank and rob them of two hundred dollars, I am just as guilty as the person who robbed them of five thousand dollars. If you

did as much for another person as God has done for you and he or she robbed you every week, how much respect would you have for him or her? Bring Him all that you owe Him. "Into the storehouse that there may be meat in My house..."

III: Consecrated Place

This is why the tithe should not be taken to Sam's, Office Max, Office Depot, Dillard's, or Target. When we bring the tithe to His house, all the needs of the congregation will be met from our collective resources.

"Prove Me now in this, and see if I will not open to you the windows of heaven and pour you out a blessing that you will not have room enough to receive."

IV: Constant Provisions

Whatever you need, God is able to pour it out. That is what He did for us with Jesus Christ. He gave us a gift that has more grace than we have room to receive. He died for us, was buried for us, and He rose from the grave with all power in His hands.

Do I need to say any more? Let's get this matter of the tithe right, and let's do it RIGHT NOW!

CHAPTER 17

WORKING WITH THE RIGHT TOOLS

1 Corinthians 3:9–13
STEWARDSHIP

I n May of 1974, I had the joy of walking across the stage at the Music Hall in Houston, Texas, with more than 350 other classmates, as I graduated and received my high school diploma from Booker T. Washington High School. A few weeks after graduation, my father walked into my room and asked me what my plans were for my future. I informed him that I had enrolled in trade school to become a sheetrock finisher, which is a skill I am still able to use until this day. My father then shared with me how proud he was with the changes that I had made in my life, and how I was now placing myself in a position to be able to adequately provide for myself financially.

After enrolling in that trade school, one of the first things that we were taught about sheetrock finishing was the importance of making sure that we had all the tools that we would need for every job. A few of the basic tools included a six-inch knife for the fundamental taping and spotting of nails. We needed a four-inch knife for small areas and around door jams. We needed a ten-inch knife for the top coat of the sheetrock mud, which was called a floating knife. We needed a twelve-inch knife for the finish coat of the sheetrock mud, which was called a skimming knife. Then we needed a sheetrock mud pan that could be attached to our hips while we were working. There were also some other tools that were helpful, and all of them were listed on a sheet of paper for every student. The instructor emphasized to us the importance of making sure that we keep our tools with us in the trunk of our automobile at all times, because we never knew when a call would come for us to go out on a job. If we did not have our tools, the company would simply call somebody else, and they would receive the financial rewards from the job instead.

I also remember one of the students in the class complaining about how much the tools cost. The instructor politely said to him, "You have a choice; you can invest in the tools that you will need and learn how to use them and then be able to provide for yourself for the rest of your life. Or, you can choose not to invest the money needed for the tools and spend the rest of your life hoping that somebody will give you a free handout."

As I reflect on this memory, it helps me tremendously in placing what Paul says to us in this passage in its proper perspective. Here in these verses, Paul gives us some precious insight on the fact that every person who is a part of the body of Christ should be doing at least three basic things. We should be *watering* what has been planted, we should be *working* together for the glory of God, and we need to be *warned* of the danger of trying to do what we do for the Lord with no tools or with the wrong tools.

God does not expect us to fulfill the assignments that He has placed before us by using the tools that we have received from the world and by using only secular reasoning and rational. Many of us who are a part of the church have the same complaint that one of the students in my class in trade school had more than thirty-seven years ago. He complained about how much the tools cost without realizing the fact that the tools were going to be the means that he could use to work with in order to receive what he would need to financially sustain himself.

Many Christians are not growing in their faith because they are only focusing on what the cost seems to be when it comes to our relationship with the Lord. We think the cost of a dime from every dollar, which is the tithe, is too high, but we fail to realize that God has promised that if we would pay Him what we owe Him, then He will open the windows of heaven and pour us out a blessing that we would not have room enough to receive. We think that the cost of Sunday school attendance, Bible study time, and the effort required for being involved in a ministry are too high. But we fail to realize is these are the tools that can help us from being deceived, dissuaded, distracted, and destroyed by the devil.

I want you to take just a moment before you read any further in this chapter and ask yourself a few questions: What kind of tools am I working with, who gave them to me, and do I really know how to use them to the glory of God? As a leader of the Lord's people, I have discovered that many of us are experts when it comes to using the tools that we have picked up in the world. Women know how to use the tools of talking a man out of his money. Men know how to use the tools of talking a lady out of her purity. We know how the use the tools of walking in a certain way to get somebody's attention. We know how to use the tool of lying to say the check is in the mail, and we don't even have a checking account. We know how to use the tools of making up phony excuses for not being involved in the work of the church. Then on the other hand, we claim that we don't have a good study Bible, because they cost too much, and yet we manage to find money to do those things that satisfy our flesh and give us a level of temporary pleasure.

Right here in this text, Paul is trying to get us to understand that if we are going to live the kind of lives that make a difference in the kingdom of God, we need to make sure that we are not trying to work for the Lord empty-handed or with the tools that we have found in the world. Paul gives us the key to this whole matter in verses 9 and 10 when he says, "For we are God's fellow workers; you are God's field; you are God's building. According to the grace of God which was given to me as a wise master builder, I have laid the foundation, and another builds on it. But let each one take heed how he builds on it."

After I read this verse prayerfully and carefully, the light came on in my mind, and the Holy Spirit revealed to me that He is calling to our attention the need to fulfill:

I: Our Individual Assignments

Paul gives us at least three labels of identification here in verse 9. Then he gives us a warning and an assignment in verse 10. He says we are God's fellow workers, we are God's field, and we are God's building. Take just a moment to really analyze this carefully. The fact that we are laborers together with God means that we should be using our *energy*. The fact that we are God's field means that we should be *examples* of the One who has planted Himself in us. Then the fact that we are God's building means that we have been *edified* by God. Now let me make that block one more time. I'll drive a little slower on this trip. This elevated my mind to heights of spiritual erudition. It caused me to consider that God has chosen to work with me.

I know you may feel like God should be honored to have you working for Him. But when I first consider my sinful past, scornful activities, and weaknesses and consider the fact that despite the shame that I have brought to His name, despite the many times I have failed Him, disappointed Him, and disrespected Him and realize He still has chosen to work with me, it just blows my mind. This is especially true when I consider that He was not forced to work with me but has purposefully chosen to work with me.

Well, maybe you still don't understand. So allow me to phrase it like this. There are some people who are reading this book right now, and the only reason you are not really connected and committed to a church is because there are some people that you just don't feel like you can work with. You think that they are not good enough, not smart enough, not holy enough, and not morally pure enough. But I thank the Lord for the fact that He does not feel about some of us the way some of us feel about ourselves. The Lord also wants us to know that even though we have been chosen by Him, it does not mean that we don't have any responsibilities. Paul says we are "His fellow workers." This means that we all should be doing some work. Not only are we the Lord's coworkers, but we are also His field.

This brought to my attention the fact that whatever grows in our lives is a good sign of whom we are allowing to plant in our lives. Let's pause parenthetically right here and ask ourselves what kind of fruit we are producing in the field of our lives. How much Bible knowledge is growing up in you? How much forgiveness is growing up in you? How much holy living is growing up in you? How much fruit of the spirit is growing up in you? And how much liberal giving is growing up in you as a result of the seeds that you have planted in the kingdom of God? Our lives should be walking, living, and breathing examples of the kinds of seeds that have been planted in us. Are you an easily recognizable field? Or, do people have to do a double take to determine if you are a child of the world or a child of God? We should be using our *energy* for the Lord, we should be *examples* of the Lord, and we should be placing ourselves in position to be *edified* by the Lord. We are God's building.

If I were preaching at Grace Tabernacle, I would ask the congregation to "lean in real close" for this next statement. When Paul says "we are God's field" that means He cultivates us and fertilizes us. But as God's building, that means that He now LIVES IN US! So I need to ask the question, what kind of house do you have the Lord living in? We are His temple and are the dwelling place of His precious Holy Spirit. This helps us to recognize that we need to be careful about the things we allow our minds and our lives to become polluted with. Paul says, "I have laid the foundation, and someone else builds on it, but each one of us needs to be careful what we place both on the Lord's land, and in the Lord's house which is our body."

I feel like an infomercial salesman right here. But wait, there's more! In verses 11 and 12, we are privileged to read these inspired words: "For no other foundation can anyone lay than that which is laid, which is Jesus Christ. Now if anyone builds on this foundation with gold, silver, precious stones, wood, hay, straw…" The Holy Spirit is bringing our attention to the fact that as believers in Jesus Christ we also have an:

II: Investment Assurance

One of the first questions that most people who make investments ask is, "How safe is my investment going to be?" Some of you may want to know, if I surrender my life and my resources to Jesus, and if I throw away my old worldly tools and invest in His tools, how safe will my investment be? Now, before I answer that question, I need to make us aware that Paul is informing us of the truth that if we are a part of the church that Jesus Christ died for at Calvary and was raised from the grave for, we do not need a new foundation. We just need better building materials and more committed workers to build on the unbreakable foundation that was laid more than two thousand years ago. This foundation has not cracked, it has not shifted, it has not settled, and it has not been broken. So if you want to know if the investments of your time, talent, and treasure are safe, the answer is, ain't no doubt about it!

I want you to notice the extreme contrast of materials listed here in verse 12. He begins with the valuable things; he calls them gold, silver, and precious stones. Then he moves on to the worthless materials; he calls those things wood, hay, and straw. Now, I need your attention because there is a question we must ask ourselves before we move any further: Has God done enough for you to receive your gold? Has His Son done enough to receive your silver? And is His peace worth your precious stones? Many of us make the mistake of giving the grocery store our best gold. We give the shopping mall our best silver, and a part-time lover our precious stones. What kind of materials are you using in your work for the kingdom of God? Are you using materials that are permanent, beautiful, valuable, and hard to obtain, like gold, silver, and precious stones? Or, are you using materials that are temporary, ordinary, cheap, and easy to obtain, like wood, hay, and straw? How much of your quality time does the Lord receive? When was the last time you gave the Lord some money that you really wanted to keep for yourself? When was the last time that you made a sacrifice for Him and made yourself available to help somebody to grow in his or her walk with Jesus Christ, even if it caused you to have to come out of your comfort zone?

There is a song we would sing when I was a young boy that featured the phrase "only what you do for Christ will last." We need to be reminded of a major truth, which is whenever we make an investment into the kingdom of God, we are investing in our eternity and in the eternity of the people that we work with in the church. In this passage, Paul also helps us understand that the Lord gives us a choice as to the kinds of materials that we use in our work for Him. He is not going to force you to give Him your gold, silver, and precious stones, but I do need to tell you that if all you are using is wood, hay, and straw, you really have a problem. Because wood will rot, hay will be destroyed in a storm, and straw will be easily blown away. Could this be the reason some people don't have any lasting power in their work for the Lord, because they are using the wrong kinds of building materials? (Just food for thought.)

In verse 13, we read these life-changing and liberating words: "Each one's work will become clear; for the Day will declare it, because it will be revealed by fire; and the fire will test each one's work, of what sort it is." This helped me understand that we must all be prepared for the:

III: The Inspector's Appraisal

Whatever we do for the Lord will one day face His Divine inspection. Before you can close on a home purchase, there must be an inspection to determine if the property is worth what they are selling it for. Paul says, "Each one's work will become clear; for the Day will declare it, because it will be revealed by fire; and the fire will test each one's work, of what sort it is." Now let me do my best to help each one of us apply this verse to our every day lives.

This verse helps me understand that there will be a day of public declaration that will reveal our private development and will allow us to maintain our permanent determination. Let's read that again.

"Each person's work will become clear...," and there is coming a specific day when God will reveal to the whole world what our true motives were for doing what we do in the kingdom of God and for those things that we should be doing and are not doing.

The manner that the Lord will expose the pure from the pretenders is by allowing us to be exposed to the test of fire. Going through the fire refers to when we show how much we are dedicated to the Lord, and our dedication leads to our development from Lord. The fire will test us and our work will be revealed after we come out of the fire. We will never build up our determination until we have gone through the fire. If you will begin to trust the Lord with a greater amount of your resources to invest in His kingdom and in the lives of other people, the Lord will begin to put out some fires in your life that you have been trying to handle all by yourself. Just trust Him and watch Him honor His word.

CHAPTER 18

BLESSED TO BE A BLESSING

Genesis 45:4–7
STEWARDSHIP

The life of Joseph is arguably one of the most interesting, intriguing, and heartwarming stories in all of the Old Testament. Joseph was the eleventh son born to his father, Jacob. He was the first son that Jacob had with the woman that he loved with his whole heart, and her name was Rachel. We are introduced to him in Genesis Chapter 30, and his story continues until the end of the book in Genesis Chapter 50. His mother Rachel had been barren for many years. She had been dealing with the stigma of not being able to have any children because of her unfruitful, biological condition, but in the midst of it all, she never lost her hope, and she never gave up on God. She knew in her heart that God would come through in His own time, and that is exactly what He did.

Genesis Chapter 30 verses 22–24 tell us that "God remembered Rachel, and God listened to her and opened her womb. And she conceived and bore a son, and said, 'God has taken away my reproach.' So she called his name Joseph and said, 'The Lord will add to me another son.'" Now there is something amazing in this story that caught my attention, and I want to share it with you. Notice carefully what happened in the mind of Rachel. It was after many years of emotional pain, and personal frustration from not being able to have a child. Then as soon as God blesses her with her first child, she has a level of faith in God to believe that God is not through blessing her. This level of faith is exemplified in what she names her first son. The name Joseph means, "The Lord will add."

And I believe that we who claim to have faith in God must get to a point in our lives where we start to realize a very important fact: no matter how much pain we have had to deal with in the past does not preclude, prevent, hinder, stagnate, detour, dissuade, distract, cancel, or stop God from blessing us in the future. We must get to a level in our faithful expectations where we start to believe God for His very best no matter what the devil may have done to us in the earlier phases of our lives. You may be dealing with some struggles and difficulties right now, but you need to be reassured that if you will just hold on, God's best for your life is yet to come.

And in Genesis Chapter 35, this is what the Lord allowed Rachel to experience. God blessed her to give birth to another son whose name was Benjamin, just before she dies and goes to live in the presence of the almighty God.

But it was Rachel's first son, Joseph, who is the focus for this chapter. This young man grew up with God's favor on his life. He also had an inflated ego, and he was very self-centered. He was a young man who was blessed by God, but he had to be taught by God why He had chosen to bless him.

> **I have discovered that there are many people who have been blessed by God, but the problem lies in that they think all that God has given to them is for them.**

They never discover the principle that God always blesses us through other people, that God uses us to be a blessing to other people, and that He does not give us the right to choose whom He will bless through us. We find this principle revealed with spiritual clarity in the words of Jesus found in Luke 6:38. There we read these words: "Give, and it shall be given to you, good measure, pressed down, shaken together, and running over shall MEN GIVE into your bosom." The Lord blesses our lives through the lives of other people. And this was a principle that Joseph had to go through a whole lot in his life to get clear in his mind.

Allow me to give you a brief synopsis of some of the things that Joseph went through. He was blessed by God to be a visionary dreamer, and then he made the mistake of sharing his dreams with his brothers, who hated him. His father, Jacob, made him a multicolored coat, and while he was parading in the garment before his brothers, they kidnapped him, stole his coat, threw him in a pit, and told his father that he had been killed by a wild animal. Then his brothers returned to the scene of the crime and sold him into slavery to some Ishmaelites.

While he was in prison, God gave him favor with a baker and a butler. He had the gift of interpreting dreams. He gave an explanation to both of these men concerning their dreams, but when the butler was released from prison, he forgot all about Joseph for two years until Pharaoh had a dream. Then he told the king that there was a man in prison who could help him to understand his dream. The Bible tells us that Pharaoh brought Joseph out of the prison, and the Lord favored him at every turn in his life.

Next, Joseph had an encounter with the wife of a man named Potifar. She accused him of trying to rape her because he had refused her sexual advances. We are told that Joseph ran away from her, and he lost his *coat*, but he did not lose his *character*. After spending some additional time in prison, God allowed him to once again find favor in the eyes of Pharaoh, and he became the number two man in charge of the entire nation of Egypt.

It was not long after that that a famine set up in the land of Canaan, where Joseph's father and his brothers, who had sold him into slavery, were living. The only place where they could buy food was in Egypt. These brothers did not know that Joseph was still alive, but God knew. Jacob sent them to Egypt without realizing that they were going to the man whom they had caused much hurt and harm to. When his brothers came to Egypt, Joseph was an opulently rich man and was extremely powerful. After a few days of concealing his true identity, we arrive at the main focus for this chapter. Here in Genesis Chapter 45 is when Joseph makes his brothers aware that he was the brother that they had sold into slavery. Despite everything that he had gone through, God still had a purpose for his life, and there was a reason why God had allowed all that he had been forced to deal with. Joseph says to his brothers in verse 5 of Chapter 45: "But now, do not therefore be grieved or angry with yourselves because you sold me here; for God sent me before you to preserve life." This verse helps us understand how Joseph was able to:

I: Put His Past Pain in the Proper Perspective

Joseph learned that there are some things in life that happen to us, and we will never be able to make humanistic sagacity out of them. There are times when we will go through things that are totally unreasonable, illogical, and almost asinine. We will have more questions than answers, more pain than relief, more bad memories, than precious memories, and more sleeplessness than restfulness.

> **So when we face those difficult seasons, we need to release that pain, get rid of that "get-even mentality," and learn how to make the best of what God has left us to work with.**

In other words, there are some things that we just need to learn how to get over and move on. Because the bottom line to the whole matter is, if God allowed it, He had a purpose for it whether we like it or not. And we can make a choice to allow that pain to make us better or to make us bitter. It has happened, it has been done, and it cannot be undone. We cannot erase it, eradicate it, obliterate it, or eliminate it. We don't have the luxury of a Hollywood director who can say, "Take one, take two, or, shoot that scene over." Once the pain is there, it is there. The only question is how are we going to deal with it? We can either grow from it or be stunted by it and remain in the same old negative, mean, cold condition of unforgiveness that has held us captive for many months and years.

When you read this story, you never find Joseph asking his brothers questions like, why did you do this to me? Did you think that I deserved this? Why on earth would you lie to our father and tell him that I was dead? Did you all even think about trying to come and find me? No, Joseph does not ask any of those questions, but he does say, "For God sent me here to preserve life." In other words, Joseph recognized that God had used all that he had gone through not only to give food to his hungry brothers and his father, but to also have the foresight to develop and implement a food conservation plan that made sure that the people in Egypt and all of their neighbors could come there and buy food during this time of famine.

All this helped me to understand that the best way to find relief from your past pain is to start focusing on helping somebody else. Whatever you are going through, be assured that God has a purpose for the pain of your past. And the sooner you learn to release your past pain, you will become better equipped to handle your future assignments. There are so many women who cannot treat their present husband or the man who is a part of their lives in the right way now because they are still holding on to the pain some other man has caused them. Some men will not shower their wives with gifts and affection simply because the last wife or last woman was a gold digger. The person you are connected to now is not him or her! And if you are not over that past pain, the fault also lies with you because a new relationship should never have been started until the healing process was complete.

Joseph's life helps us to understand that we will never receive our twenty-first century blessing from God as long as we are harboring twentieth century pain and bitterness.

As we move further in the story, we notice these words in verse 6: "For these two years the famine has been in the land, and there are still five years in which there will be neither plowing nor harvesting." Because Joseph's past pain was in the proper perspective, it gave him the mental and spiritual freedom to begin making:

II: Proper Plans for His Present Predicament

(I must say WOW to that myself.) Joseph informs his brothers that the difficult days are not over. But if we stick together, we can make it.

This is the main problem that I have with all of these so-called prophets of prosperity. They tell us about God's favor and God's blessings, and they tell us about claiming the promises of Abraham. They tell us to believe it and receive it, name it and claim it, call it and haul it, grab it and have it. But no one says anything about the recession that would attack our finances, the cutbacks that would attack our jobs, the cancer that would attack our bodies, the divorce that would attack our marriages, the repossessions that would attack our cars, the foreclosure that would attack our homes, the dropouts that would attack our schools, the drugs that would attack our children, the violence that would attack our neighborhoods, the back-stabbing that would attack our friendships, and divisiveness that would attack our churches. Joseph wants his brothers to know that all the difficult days are not over. He does not want them to think that simply because they have chosen to come to him for help that they will not have to make some sacrifices in the future. But he also wants them to know that if they would stick together, they can make it through this together.

The reason I can say this is because when you read on further in the story, you will discover that in order for these brothers to keep their families alive during this famine, they had to move from Canaan to Egypt. Canaan is the place that God wanted them to be, but Egypt was the place that they would later be freed from. This lets me know that whenever we mistreat people, God just may temporarily relocate us from where He wants us to be to teach us that the people whom we caused the most harm to just may be the ones that He will use to bail us out during difficult times in our lives. Joseph says to his brothers they still have five more years of this famine and will not be able to do any plowing or any harvesting. But he says in essence, "We can make it, if we all learn to stick together." They had to learn how to use wisely what God had given them to work with. We must learn how to be good stewards and exercise the same principles.

When we do this, we will be able to make it when hard times set in. God never intended for us to spend everything we make and to live from paycheck to paycheck. I try to get people to understand that when you have not treated God right and paid Him the tithe when you had a job, and when you have not been fair with those people who represent God, no matter how much you may not like them personally, God just may allow you to suffer some unnecessary consequences for your behavior. Don't ever make the mistake of feeling like you will never need the help of another person, because you never know where life will take you. God will make us eat those same words, and we may find ourselves on the begging end and not on the giving end.

Finally, in verse 7, Joseph says, "And God sent me before you to preserve a posterity for you in the earth and to save your lives by a great deliverance." Joseph learned how to put his past pain in the proper perspective; he learned how to make proper plans for his present predicament, and finally he learned the importance of:

III: Properly Planting for the Posterity of Other People

This just a fancy way of saying that Joseph did not eat his seed. He planted his seed, because he knew that later during the time of famine he would get hungry. By planting his seed, he not only had enough for right now, but he also had enough for himself, Pharaoh, other servants, the nation of Egypt, and now even for 11 brothers, all of their wives and children, and his father to eat.

> Joseph did not have a selfish mentality. He was looking for a way to be a blessing to somebody else other than always looking out for himself.

Notice what he says: "God sent me before you to preserve posterity for you in the earth." Whenever your number one concern is about blessing somebody else, God will always make sure that you are blessed. (Got it yet?) When you give enough on Sunday to keep the lights on at the house of the Lord, God will make sure your lights stay on at your house. (Is it clear yet?) When you give enough so that the transportation ministry at your church will be able to buy gas for the church vans, God will always make sure that you have gas in your cars. (Okay, I think you see where I'm headed) When you give enough so that your church can give away free food, God will make sure that you have food on your table for you and your family.

My minister of music, Brother Jerry Perry, helped me to understand a tremendous principle in this story. He asked me, "Pastor, did the faithfulness of Joseph initiate the favor of God, or did the faithfulness of God initiate the favor in Joseph's life?" We see two prominent principles at work here in this story. We see favor and faithfulness, and we need to know which one came first. And the answer to that question is God's faithfulness came first. The reason I know this is true is because the answer is found in Romans 5:8: "But God demonstrated His love toward us, in that while we were yet sinners Christ died for us."

Joseph used what he had to be a blessing to somebody else, and this is exactly what Jesus did. God blessed Jesus with some blood. He decided not to keep the blood for Himself, but to use that blood to be a blessing to somebody else. When Jesus died for us, He gave us His blood. Joseph gave his brothers bread, but Jesus gave us His blood. He died for us, and when He was raised from the grave, God never had a need to give Him any more blood, because He had used the blood to be a blessing to somebody else. When we use what God has given us to bless somebody else, He will make sure that all of our needs are met.

CHAPTER 19

Overcoming Impossibilities with Insufficiencies

1 Kings 17:8–16
Stewardship

I realize that the subject I have chosen for this chapter seems to present an obvious oxymoron, a puzzling paradox, and some may even think that it is bordering on asininity. The educated and logical mind would lead us to think that there cannot possibly be any significant connection between overcoming our impossible situations by using our insufficient resources. On the surface, they seem to be mutually exclusive terms. Many of us think that if we are going to overcome our unfeasible predicaments, we need a massive amount of resources. I will agree that these assessments are true from a humanistic and practical perspective. But on the other side of the equation, some of us are a part of the Body of Christ and know about *God's ability* to take what seems to be little to nothing, and how He turns it into an overwhelming abundance—only after we take it out of our hands and place it in His hands.

I believe that many of us can testify that at one time or another in our lives, we seemed to be in an impossible situation. Some of those situations were self-imposed. Some were because of poor and irrational choices we made. Some were because of hasty decisions; some were because we were manipulated and deceived, and others simply came in our direction with seemingly no explanation at all. I think this would be a good time for me to share a little secret with us that the Lord has shared with me. The secret is that whenever a Christian is faced with a situation in which we cannot figure out what God is doing, it is usually because God is about to do something that will literally blow our minds.

God purposely chooses not to tell us all about it in advance, because He wants to strengthen our faith while we are going through the difficulty and then teaches us how to trust in Him and in Him alone. When the financial storm settles, and when the economic winds calm down, the Lord also wants us to learn the importance of giving Him unrestrained and spontaneous praise. In many instances, when we read this story, or hear it preached, we have a tendency to compartmentalize it into a story only about giving money to the preacher, the man of God, and then waiting for a miracle. But there is so much more housed here in this wonderful scenario. This is not a fairytale; this is not a metaphor or an analogy.

This was a real story about a real prophet named Elijah, a real woman, a real son, and a real drought, and they were about to experience real death. This is not only a story about giving money to God; even more important it's also about having faith in God, being obedient to God, waiting on God, and trusting God to open a new window when every other door seems to be closed.

I have discovered that when many of us are facing impossible situations, we often give up, quit, throw in the towel, and wave the white flag of surrender. You may be reading this chapter while you are going through something that appears to be too difficult for you to handle all by yourself. You may need to start by becoming more committed to Christ with a greater level of connection to your local church. But you are hesitant to make a move because you are focusing more on what you don't have as opposed to being willing to work with what you do have. Many people have not surrendered their lives and their resources to the Lord, because in their minds they think they are too far removed from God to be restored by His grace. But the very fact that you are reading this book is proof positive to the truth that God loves you and cares about you, because if He did not, He would not have even allowed you to have eyes to read with so He could move your faith and your stewardship to a new level.

Why not read this chapter with a determination to apply the principles, which are from the Bible. I want to challenge you to make up your mind that this will be your day of deliverance. This is your day of liberation. This is your day of transition from a sideline spectator of ministry to a committed participator in ministry. There are some valuable lessons we can learn from God in this story about Elijah and this widow from Zarephath.

When we take a moment to digress from the text in Chapter 17, we will discover in verse 7 that the brook that the Lord had been allowing Elijah to drink from during this season of drought, suddenly dried up. It would seem rational to me that God would send Elijah to a fertile place of abundant food and a constant supply of water to reward him for his faithfulness during this period of his life. But instead God sends a hungry and thirsty prophet to the home of a broke widow woman who also had a young son.

Now, just in case you may be wondering, how is God able to bring us to the level of meeting our impossibilities with our insufficiencies? The first clue is found right here in verse 9. The Lord tells Elijah to go to the widow's house because He has commanded her to provide for him there. The Hebrew word for "commanded" literally means to "set in order." I want you to know that it matters not what our personal predicament may be:

I: The Lord Recognizes our Situations

The Lord was not oblivious to the condition of this widow, and the Lord is not unaware of what is going on in your life, no matter how severe it may seem to be. The reason I know this is true is because He has allowed you to be reading this chapter just when you need confirmation, hope, and encouragement from Him. Perhaps you may be thinking that your circumstances are more difficult than what this woman was facing. Well, let's keep reading. This widow had an *extreme emotional situation*. She and her son were about to die. She also thought that she was going to have to watch her child die right before her very eyes. Are there any things that seem to be about to die out in your life? When we face these emotions, it causes us to attempt to take matters into our own hands and ignore what the Lord is saying.

This widow also had an *extreme economic situation.* They were about to eat their last meal and die. Let me help you to put this in its proper perspective. If you were a farmer who owned barns, wheat fields, multiple crops, livestock, and farming equipment, and a tornado came and destroyed everything you owned except for a jar of seed, would you have more success in rebuilding you life by eating the seed or planting the seed? The answer is obviously "planting the seed."

Have you ever wondered why, after the devil has caused a tornado to blow through our finances and we are down to our last ten, twenty or fifty dollars, we will not plant it in the kingdom of God, but we will go out and eat it up at a restaurant or at the grocery store? Is it possible that the main reason we are not able to recover from a financial storm is because we are eating seed that we should be planting? (Just some food for thought—no pun intended.)

When we give to the Lord and to those who represent the Lord, all we are doing is planting seeds in the eternal kingdom of God. Why plant your seeds in an unfertile field when God wants you to place them in His hands? Many of us claim that we love God more than we love anything and anybody else, but it is not always reflected in how we give to Him and how much of our lives we trust Him with. What do you have with you today that is too good or too much to trust God with? If you say nothing, what is causing you not to trust Him with all of it?

This widow also had an *extreme educational situation.* The reason I call this an extreme educational situation is because what Elijah tells her to do really does not make sense. Logic 101 would say don't do it. First grade reasoning would say don't do it. Grade school common sense would say don't even think about it. But God often challenges us to do what seems to be irrational and erratic, so that we might experience the impossible. Allow me to give you a few examples. Marching around a city's walls once a day for six days and then seven times on the seventh day does not make sense, but it did lead to victory. A teenage shepherd boy going out to fight a nine-foot tall giant does not make sense, but it did lead to victory. Going across a Red Sea with no boats, floats, or life jackets does not make sense, but it did lead to victory. Giving money to the Lord when you need money to pay your own bills does not seem to make sense, but it will lead to victory.

This also exposes us to an additional truth. It is one that many of us are slow to embrace, but it is necessary for our spiritual development in the area of our stewardship. That principle is:

II: The Lord Requires Our Sacrifices

Notice what happens in this story. The Lord purposely sent this prophet in need to this widow in need to show both of them His ability to meet their collective needs. (WOW!) Let me take a praise break right here, I'll return in just a moment.

Let's consider the intricate details of the story. In verse 10, Elijah asks this woman to bring him some water in a cup, and then in verse 11, he tells her to bring him a piece of bread in her hand. Notice how the woman responds in verse 12. She says, "As the Lord your God lives, I do not have bread only a handful of flour in a bin and a little oil in a jar." Now, I am not a culinary specialist, but I do know that you cannot make bread without flour! But the thing that the Lord is trying to expose us to is that this woman did not have any bread, but she does have the ingredients to make the bread. That is where the problem lies with many of us. We focus more on what we don't have and completely overlook what the Lord has given us to work with.

You may not have a solo, but you do have a soprano, alto, or tenor voice that could help the choir. You may not have a thousand dollars to give to your church at one time, but you do have 10 percent that you could give each week to support the work of the Lord. You may not have the ability to lead a ministry, but you do have the ability to be a part of a ministry.

The Lord wants us to learn how to use what we have to His glory and to trust Him for the results. If there is something in your hands that seems like it is about to die, you have found the answer to bringing it back to life. Take it out of your unfertile hands and place it in God's productive hands. This woman tells Elijah that she has been gathering sticks so that she can cook her last meal and *then she and her son will die.* Then, in verse 13, Elijah tells her not to fear, but to make him a *cake first* and then make one for herself and her son. I did not go to school long, but I was there on the day when they taught us that there cannot be a *first* without a *second*. So when he tells her to cook for him first, that gave her the confidence to know that her miracle was on the way. Because, all she thought she had was enough for two people, and already Elijah is telling her that God will provide for at least three people. The Lord is waiting for us to make the sacrifice and watch Him step in and work a miracle. But our problem is housed in the fact that we want to eat the cake and disobey God and still expect Him to work the miracle.

I'm sure you are wondering, as I was, how this story ends. Well, let's keep reading because we are about to discover how:

III: The Lord Will Release His Sufficiency

In verses 15 and 16, we find these words: "So she went away and did according to the word of Elijah; and she and he and her household ate for many days. The bin of flour was not used up, nor did the jar of oil run dry, according to the word of the Lord which He spoke by Elijah." Let's say it together. "God will provide for His children. He will protect His children, and all His children have to do is to be willing to trust His with the little that we have."

God is able to meet your impossible situations when we learn how to place our insufficiencies in His hand. I don't know what you have, but I do know that what you need is more than what you have. Just release it by faith and turn it over into the hands of the Lord, because His hands are bigger than your hands. We can overcome our impossibilities with insufficiencies when we trust the Lord with the little that we have.

CHAPTER 20

GIVING TO GOD IN A COMPLICATED TIME

Jonah 2: 7–10
STEWARDSHIP

When it comes to this matter of giving to God, most of us only want to talk about it and think about it when things are going well in our lives. The devil has led us astray and tricked us into believing that when we are facing tough financial times, we must strive to pay everybody else first and then give God the crumbs and scraps of what we have left. I believe I stand on safe ground when I say we all have had periods of extreme difficulty in our lives. And the real truth of the matter is that many of us are still experiencing some strenuous and ominous seasons of emotional and financial upheaval right now. But I think I am also safe when I say that there is not a person who will read this book who has ever faced a situation as difficult as the one in the life of Jonah.

Because of Jonah's insubordination and his determination to do things his way as opposed to doing them God's way, he found himself swallowed up and in the belly of a great fish. He was thrown overboard by some passengers from a ship that he never should have been on in the first place. And I think this would be a good place for me to pause and ask the question, When was the last time you challenged God, and it led to something meaningful and significant and brought you true peace and happiness?

There are many believers who attend worship each week, and they hear their pastors challenge them to "pay the tithe and give an offering." But they have chosen to handle God's money their own ways, and it seems like the financial sinkhole is getting deeper and deeper. We need to stop a moment to consider that God does not command us to give to Him because He needs what we have. God commands us to give to Him because He knows that He not only has what we need, but He is all that we need. If you seem to be swallowed up by debt and are overcome with financial obligations, and you seem to be only a matter of days from drowning, don't give up. I have come to tell you that there is still hope.

Jonah shows us in this text what our number one financial priority should be. When we read this prayer of Jonah here in chapter 2, we do not read about him asking God for deliverance. This whole prayer is an admission of his rebelliousness. He was determined to do things his way. The Lord told him to go to Nineveh and preach. Instead he decided to go to Joppa and catch a boat to Tarshish in an attempt to flee from the presence of the Lord. The very thought of trying to flee from the presence of the Lord is filled with excessive asininity. How on earth can a person think that they can run from the presence of the Lord? The Bible tells us that God is everywhere at the same time. Whenever He turns around, He bumps into Himself. He is from everlasting to everlasting, which means He is always going to the place that He just came from. Whenever God slides over, He sits in His own lap, and God is the only person who has the answer even before we know what the question is.

He told Moses to tell the people, "I am that I am hath sent thee." This speaks to the eternal *isness* of God. (It's my book; I can make up words as I choose to do so.) He has no was. He has no will be. He is older than time and longer than eternity.

Despite all this, Jonah still tried to run away from the Lord. You can run from God, but you cannot hide from God. David cleared that matter up in Psalm 139:7 when he asked, "Where can I go from Your Spirit, or where can I flee from Your presence? If I ascend into heaven, Thou are there, If I make my bed in hell, behold You are there. If I take the wings of the morning and dwell to the uttermost parts of the sea, even there Your hand shall lead me and Your right hand shall hold me."

So here is Jonah in the belly of a great fish, and he perhaps he is thinking that his days are numbered. He knows that he has no one to blame but himself. Before I move into the meat of this chapter, allow me to digress a moment and share with you a sacred slice of scripture that will give us something significant to shout about. Grab your Bible and look at verse 17 of Chapter 1. There we read, "Now the Lord had prepared a great fish to swallow Jonah."

This helped me understand that God is so merciful, He even protects us while He is punishing us.

You see, whenever a person would be thrown overboard in the middle of the sea, they would be quickly eaten up by ferocious and bloodthirsty sharks. But God had a great fish in place to swallow up Jonah before the sharks could get to him. May I pull off to the side of the road right here? Instead of us complaining about the things that have us swallowed up right now at this point in our lives, we need to learn how to thank God for the fact that He did not allow the sharks to get us. Trouble may have you right now, but you need to thank God for not allowing the trouble to kill you.

Well, I wanted to know, how can you find yourself in the belly of a great fish, surrounded by water, weeds, and impending death, and you take the time to say to God, "I will sacrifice to You With the voice of thanksgiving; I will pay what I have vowed. Salvation is of the Lord"? In other words, how do you think about giving to God when you need so much from God? He needed forgiveness, healing, restoration, salvation, and liberation. He needed lifting, oxygen, protection, assurance, and mercy. Well, there it is! The light just went on in my head. The time when we need to focus on giving a lot to God is when we need a lot from God!

I believe one of the reasons that Jonah was willing to give God a special offering even while he was in the belly of this great fish was because he knew in his heart that he had used God's money to buy something that he was not authorized to purchase. And if you don't believe me, just look at Chapter 1 and verse 3. It is there we are told that Jonah fled from the presence of the Lord, and he went down to Joppa, found a ship going to Tarshish, and PAID the fare to get on board.

Look at verse 2. The Lord told Jonah to arise and go to Nineveh, and whenever God sends us anywhere, He always takes care of the travel expenses. But when we travel in our own directions and make our own decisions, we wind up spending God's money in places where it was never intended to be spent. Many of us are willing to pay to disobey God, but we want pay to obey the Lord. This action led to the:

I: The Difficulty of Jonah

Notice what he says in verse 7, "When my soul fainted within me, I remembered the Lord; and my prayer went up to You in Your holy temple."

This verse seems to strongly suggest that Jonah did not realize how much he really needed the Lord until he knew how much he really needed the Lord. He says, "When my soul fainted within me, *then* I remembered the Lord." His soul seemed to have been doing just fine in Chapter 1, when he went down to Joppa. And I want us to take a moment to notice the descending spiral of Jonah's life after he refused to do what God told him to do. He went *down* from the presence of the Lord. Then he went *down* to Joppa, then he went *down* to the ship, then he went *down* to into the water, then he went *down* into the belly of the great fish, who took him *down* to the bottom of the sea. Whenever we fail to heed God's voice, life will continue to go down, down, and down. Jonah finds himself in a difficult position. But unlike many of us, he acknowledges that this whole ordeal is his fault alone. Jonah tells us that his soul fainted within him. He did not have a mind problem or a body problem. He had a soul problem.

The soul is the part of our invisible eternal anatomy that is exclusively connected to God. Whenever we fail to do what God has commanded us to do, we will always have trouble in our souls. The second part of this verse really caught my attention. Jonah says after his soul had fainted that he then remembered the Lord. And I wonder why does it take seasons of extreme difficulty to cause us to remember the Lord? Look at how much he is praying here throughout Chapter 2 and compare that to the complete absence of prayer in Chapter 1.

He goes on in this verse 7 to say, "And my prayer went up to You, into Your holy temple." While in this extreme time of difficulty, he starts to think not only about the Lord, but also about the house of the Lord. I hear people talk about how they are working too much to come to church and going through too much to come to church, but God has a way of causing some seasons of difficulty to come our way that will drive us to church. I don't know about you, but I would much rather drive myself to church under my own volition than have God to use some extreme difficulties to drive me into His house.

Jonah also recognized that he had focused his attention in the wrong direction. That is why he says in verse 8, "Those who regard worthless idols forsake their own mercy." This literary means "those who worship false gods have given up their only hope." When we place any person or anything ahead of God, we are literally forfeiting our own blessings and God's favor on our lives.

Then here in verse 9, we read these words: "But I will sacrifice to You with the voice of thanksgiving; I will pay what I have vowed. Salvation is of the Lord."

After he comes to grips with his difficulties, we are now able to get a glimpse of the:

II: The Dedication Of Jonah

Look carefully at verse 9. Jonah says: "I will pay what I have vowed." I did not go to school very long, but I was there on the day when they taught us that any word with an *"ed"* ending means the past tense. Jonah was not talking about giving God a new offering; he was talking about making good on the offering that he had promised to give and did not give. I wonder how many people there are who are a part of the Body of Christ that will make arrangements to get current with a late phone bill or a late car note, will catch up a late house note or a late light bill, and don't care about catching up on all the tithes that they have been robbing from God.

Jonah knew that his disobedience had gotten him in this mess in the first place. If we would come clean and tell the truth, we would have to admit that most of our financial problems are the result of us making decisions with our money without consulting God first. Most of the time, we get ourselves into the mess, and we want God to bail us out of the mess. Then when we get out of the mess, we bless everybody else with some of our money except for the one who bailed us out. And I have proof. Here it is. When was the last time you put a financial plan in place to pay God all the back tithe you owed to Him?

> **Jonah recognized that he had spent God's money to buy a ticket to get on a ship and go to a city that God never commanded him to spend in the first place.**

I have discovered that our real problem does not lie in the fact that we don't have any money. Our problem is that we spend the money that we do have on things that God has not authorized us to spend it on. But the real scary part of this story lies in the fact that God still has some great fish ready to swallow us up when we don't follow His instructions for our lives and when we fail to use His money to support His work.

Now I want us to notice one other thing, and then I will move on a little further. In Chapter 4, verses 1 and 2, we find out what the problem really was. After God spared Jonah's life, he went to Nineveh and preached, and all the people repented of their sins. Then Jonah became angry because he wanted God to annihilate the city; instead God showed mercy to the city. And did you not know that many of us will get upset when it looks like God is using us, and our money, to save people that we think need to be destroyed. God uses our money to feed people whom we think really don't need anything to eat. God is using our money to clothe people whom we think already have enough clothes. God is using our money to forgive some people whom we want to be condemned. So instead of giving to support the work of the church, we try to keep our money to ourselves and spend it on other things as Jonah did.

But God has a way of saving whom He is going to save, delivering whom He chooses to deliver, either with or without us. The results of our disobedience can be a price higher than we are able to pay.

In verse 10 we read, "So the Lord spoke to the fish, and it vomited Jonah on dry land. That is where we receive encouragement and hope for our desperate situations:

III: The Deliverance of Jonah

I want us to look carefully at this verse. Jonah has prayed for nine verses in this Chapter, and God does not send deliverance until he makes up his mind to pay God the vow that he had promised to give to the Lord. When we learn the real joy of spontaneous giving is when we will also discover God's true delivering power. The Bible says, "So the Lord spoke to the fish." Please don't miss that. God did not have to wrestle the fish. He did not have to catch the fish. He did not even have to open the mouth of the fish. All God did was speak to the fish. This simply means that God commanded the fish. God has the power to speak to whatever situation is holding us captive and tell it to set us free when we learn how to make Him our number one priority.

Sometimes God will allow us to stay in the situation a little longer than we are able to understand, because He does not want to release us too fast because we just may go back and do the same thing all over again. Jonah learned the importance of giving to God while he was in the belly of this great fish. If we handle the Lord's money the right way, He can protect us from going into the belly of the great fish. Just in case someone is reading this book and feels like they have been swallowed up by their situations, I want to tell you that God has power to speak a word and your deliverance will come. The reason I know this is true is because God has a good track record of speaking, and when He speaks, things start to happen. He spoke this world into existence.

He spoke to Abraham on Mt. Moriah and spared Isaac's life.

He spoke to Moses and the Red Sea parted.

He spoke again and Pharaoh and his armies were drowned.

He spoke to the sun and it stood still for one whole day.

He spoke to the walls of Jericho, and they came tumbling down

He spoke to some lions, and they became a pillow and mattress for Daniel.

He spoke to some fire and it did not burn the Hebrew boys.

Then Jesus spoke to the sea and said, "Peace; be still."

He spoke to a lame man and told him to pick up his bed and walk.

He spoke to a blind man and told him to go wash in the pool of Siloam, and he came back seeing.

All this lets me know that because Jesus can speak deliverance to my failures and deliverance to my fears, He can also speak deliverance to my finances. I have been delivered from my failures, fears, and financial struggles when I placed them all in His hands.

The Lord spoke to the fish and told it to deliver Jonah on dry land. This lets me know that God delivered him on safe ground, and he didn't even have to swim to shore. Since He loved us enough to die for us, the least we can do is tell Him thank you by giving Him a sacrificial offering.

The fish swallowed Jonah, but the fish did not digest Jonah. You may be swallowed by trouble, but thank God for the fact that you have not been digested by trouble.

That is what happened to Jesus. He was swallowed by the grave, but it could not digest Him because early one Sunday morning, He got up with all power in His hands.

CHAPTER 21

GOD'S CURE FOR BEING BROKE

2 Corinthians 9:8–11
STEWARDSHIP

I want to set the record straight by sharing with you that this is not a chapter about worldly and materialist prosperity. This chapter is not intended to imply that God proposes for everybody to be rich, live in mansions, and own airplanes. This chapter is not intended to imply that once we start giving, we will never have another day of economic complexity. This chapter is not intended to imply that God's people do not go through seasons of financial hardships and periods of fiscal difficulty. (I think you get the picture.) Instead this chapter is intended to boldly and emphatically proclaim that I do not believe that it was ever God's intent for His people to go without having all the basic needs in our lives met. Before we can even address this matter of depletion and tough seasons of financial hardships, we must begin by being honest both with the Lord and with ourselves.

We must start by admitting that most of the financial hardships we have don't have anything to do with our extravagant giving to God or the excessive amount of money that we have given in church. Most of our difficulties are usually followed by our admission that we started to rob God of the tithe during the very seasons when we should have been trusting Him the most.

These crises have not come because God has failed us. These crises have come into our lives as a result of our making decisions with our money without consulting God first. Many of us will make the decision to buy things that we know we cannot comfortably afford, and we fail to pray and ask the Lord to allow His Spirit to lead us in the right direction. Then when things don't work out, suddenly we start to pray and ask God to come and bail us out, while we are guilty of robbing Him at the same time that we are praying to Him.

The Lord wants us to recognize that we must get to a point where we trust Him to be faithful to His word and provide for all of our needs no matter how dark and dismal our economic outlook may seem to be. Did you not know that God is never glorified when His people are struggling in the area of our financial resources, because He already knows that it takes quality money to do quality ministry. God knows that we will have monetary needs, and He stands ready, willing, and able to meet all those needs.

The reason that I can make this statement is because in the Garden of Eden when God first created man, He gave him all that he would ever need to sustain himself and to provide for his daily needs. As a matter of fact, in Genesis 1:26, God gave mankind dominion over the fish of the sea, the birds of the air, and over everything that creeps on the earth. This was God's way of informing Adam that He knew he would need to eat, so He gave him a sea to fish from. He knew that he would want more than just seafood, so he gave him some birds of the air. He gave him the ability to grow fruits and vegetables, so that he could have all of his daily nutrients. God also knew that we would need clothes for our backs, so He gave Adam cattle to make leather, sheep to make wool, and worms to make silk. I want each of you reading this chapter to know that God has a plan for each of our lives, and He also has some guidelines and commandments as it pertains to the money that He allows to be placed in our hands.

One of the things many of us fail to realize is that we are not owners of anything. We are only stewards of what already belongs to God. We have no right to keep from God that which already belongs to Him. And during these times of cutbacks, layoffs, high unemployment, low job security, rising and falling stock markets, unstable gas prices, double digit inflation, recession, and just outright hard times, we need a word from the Lord more than ever before as it relates to how we should handle the money that comes into our hands. We cannot rely on the *Wall Street Journal*, we cannot rely on the S &P 500, and we cannot rely on the interest rates of our CDs and 401(k) plans. We must rely on the truth from the Word of God. God does have a cure for all of His people when it comes to this matter of *being broke*. But it will never work until we consistently apply—not just every once in a while—the principles that are housed here in our text.

Now, if you will take a deep breath and let me have your whole-hearted and undivided attention before I move into the meat of this chapter and seek to unpack the practical principles that are perfectly positioned here in this passage. We must come to either one of two conclusions. Before you spend any more of your time reading the remainder of this part of the book, we must get one thing straight and decide whether we believe God is lying here in these verses or if He is telling the truth. If you believe that He is lying, you need to mail this book back to me and ask for a refund, and I will gladly grant it. But if you are like me and believe that He is telling the truth in His Word, then you must come to the conclusion that the reason many of us are broke, busted, disgusted, always down and out, never have enough, and not only have trouble making ends meet but we can't even get them to wave at one another is because we are not applying the principles of His Word.

There is no middle ground. Many of us have been trying to do it our way, and we always find excuses as to why we don't pay God what we owe Him and our financial condition never gets any better. The Lord has given me the assignment of confronting these issues head on and making us aware that our financially broken status can start to turn around if we will only trust God and apply the principles from His Word. Do I have your attention?

Well, let's dive in headfirst. Paul says in verse 8 of 2 Corinthians Chapter 9: "And God is able to make all grace abound toward you, so that you will have all sufficiency in everything, and you may have an abundance for every good work." I call this:

I: God's Purpose for Our Money

I believe that if we are going to solve this problem of economic difficulty, which is just a fancy way of saying, being broke, we need to ask ourselves why God has given me some money in the first place, Many times, when we read this verse, we shout about the first part of the verse and fail to take into consideration the last part of the verse. The first part says, "And God is able to make all grace abound toward you, so that you will have a sufficient amount of everything that you need." And that word "sufficient" is *Ow tar-ki-ah* in Greek. It means contentment, enough to meet all of our needs, and competence.

Now, many of us start shouting right there, but the problem is we stopped reading too soon. The second part of the verse tells us why God has given us sufficiency in all things, and the reason is "so that you may have an abundance *for every good work.*" And the good work that he is referring to is the good work of the kingdom of God. Paul is saying the reason God gives His people money in the first place is for us to support the work of the kingdom of God. This is the purpose why He allows us to be blessed, and if we are not using the money for the purpose that He gave it to us for in the first place, then I am sure that God must ask Himself, why he should give us more money if we did not use it for the purpose he gave it to us for.

Look again at this verse. He says that you may have "all sufficiency in All things." Not some sufficiency, but all sufficiency. This is also God's way of saying when we give to Him first, and when we give Him the most, He will make sure that we do not lack anything that we will ever need in our lives. And I need to go back to the principle that I lifted earlier. We must believe either that God is lying or that He is telling the truth. And if we believe that He is telling the truth, the problem with our being broke does not lie with His inability to take care of us. The problem lies with our inability to trust Him.

We need to get to a point in our lives where we come to recognize that God can buy us better cars, clothes, and houses than we can afford to buy for ourselves. But He will never show us how much He has for us until we learn how to take what we have and place it in His hands.

Let me share this example with you. My son's name is Montel. At the time of writing this chapter, he is fifteen years old. Many of you would think that my son Montel had lost his mind if I took him to the mall and had five hundred dollars in my pocket to buy him whatever he wanted and all he had was fifteen dollars. The only way he could get access to my five hundred dollars was for him to give me his fifteen dollars, but he decided to hold on to it. Likewise, I believe that God feels like we are out of our minds, because many of us are living as if we don't realize that He has more money than we have. He can not only PAY ON your bills, He can PAY OFF your bills, but you will never get access to His money until you place the little bit that you do have in His hands!

Then in verse 9 we read, "As it is written, He scattered abroad. He gave to the poor. His righteousness endures forever." I call this:

II: The Passion Connected to God's Money

This is Paul's way of reminding us of the fact that everything God gives to us is not always for us. There are times when God wants to use us as one of His Faithful Fed-Ex and divine UPS delivery agents.

This is one of the reasons we have ministries at our church, Grace Tabernacle, like our Precious Rubies Ministry, Garments and Groceries from Grace, and the Back-to-School Revival where we give away school uniforms, supplies, food, shoes, backpacks, and hot lunches. This is why we have ministries like the Christmas Love of Jesus Celebration, where we have given away hundreds of bicycles, warm coats, pairs of shoes, and bags of groceries and thousands of toys. And after we have given all these items away, God always makes sure that we continue to have everything that we need. And the reason He does it is that He sees that we have a heart to be compassionate with the amount of money that He has given us to work with.

Notice what the verse says, "He scattered abroad." Not just in his neighborhood, but everywhere he goes. The blessed person is always ready to give and to plant a seed. And the Bible tells us that there is a blessing involved for those who consider the poor in their giving. In Proverbs 19:17 we read, "He who has pity on the poor lends to the Lord, and He will pay back what he has given." This is God's way of informing us that the only way we can be the ones to give *to the poor* and not be the ones who need for others to give to us *because we are poor* is for us to learn how to trust Him with what He has given us to work with. The verse ends by saying, "His righteousness endures forever."

This helps me understand that when we learn how to give at a level that is pleasing to God, we take on the righteous character of our heavenly Father, because He gave to us not because we deserved it, but because He loved us so much.

But wait, there's more! In verse 10 we read, "Now may He who supplies seed to the sower, and bread for food, supply and multiply the seed you have sown and increase the fruits of your righteousness." I call this:

III: The Planting of God's Money

Wake up! Don't start dozing now; it's about to get real exciting. If there is any one thing that this verse makes crystal clear, it is that the money God gives to us *is seed*. Seed was never made to be eaten; seed is designed to be planted. Allow me to read this verse from the Wycliffe's New Testament translation: "And God who continually supplies seed for the sower, and bread for eating, will supply you with seed and multiply it, and will cause your giving to yield a plentiful harvest." This is self-explanatory; I should be able to end the chapter right here. Notice what the text says.

God only gives seed to the SOWER! It is possible that we don't have enough seed because we are not doing enough sowing. Whenever you plant seed, you need to make sure of at least three things. You need to plant in the right *field*. You need to plant where something is growing. You need to give it to the right *farmer*. You need to make sure that he has a green thumb, and what he plants is growing. And then you need to have the right *faith* to wait on God until your harvest comes.

Many times, people get upset when they see other people who seem to have more of God's favor on their lives. But the mistake they make is they fail to take the time to consider that it could be because they are *sowing their seeds* as opposed to *eating their seeds*. If we fail to sow our seeds, it's nobody's fault but ours when we have no fruit to eat. Did you not know that the time we need to sow the most in God, is when we need the most from God! God says He will supply us with more seed, and He will not just add. He will multiply the seed that we have sown and increase the fruits of our righteousness. And this term, "increase the fruits of your righteousness," means that when we give to God, He will always make sure that we have what we want to give to Him. Too many of us in the Body of Christ are only consumed with thoughts about what we owe to other people, as opposed to thinking about what God has done for us through His Son Jesus Christ and how we owe Him everything that we have.

The problem lies in that many of us spend our money *foolishly*, and that is *ignoring* the *Word of God*. Then others, give their money to God *feebly*, that is *doubting* the *Word of God*. But there is another crowd who gives *faithfully*, and that is *Trusting the Word of God*. The question is, which crowd do you fall into?

> **This is the Lord's way of saying to us that He gives us the right to determine how much fruit He will give to us based on the amount of seed we give to Him.**

Finally, verse 11 says, "While you are enriched in everything for all liberality, which causes thanksgiving through us to God." We have considered the purpose for God giving us money, the passion we should have with God's money, and the planting of God's money. Let's conclude with the:

IV: Promise of More of God's Money

This verse in the Bible in Basic English translation, reads like this: "Your wealth being increased in everything, with a simple mind causing praise to God through us." This helps me to understand that when we give to God at a level that pleases Him at least three things will happen. First of all, we will experience His:

A) **Unlimited provision for us.** The verse says He will increase everything that we need.

159

B) **Unnecessary pride in us.** The Bible in Basic English says we should have a simple mind. This means we don't have to go around bragging about what we own and how much we own.

C) **Unrestrained praise from us.** Notice how the verse ends, "which cause thanksgiving through us to God." Not just your cars and your house, but thank Him that His Son died for us and then early one Sunday morning, He got up from the grave with all power. You don't have to be broke another day of your life. Just trust God and watch Him keep His word.

That's my story, and I'm sticking to it.

It is my hope and desire that you were blessed as a result of reading this book. I consider it a great honor to be used by the Lord in such a way and an even greater privilege to be able to share this information with you. As I pass it on to you, I hope that you will use it to be more prepared to live a life that pleases Him. The principles and promises that the Lord shared with me were designed to help you live a life that will make a difference in the Kingdom of God.

God has provided what we need to be properly equipped to live a successful life in Him. Now it is our responsibility to use that equipment effectively as indicated in the areas of surrendering, service, and stewardship. God has done His part.

Now, let's go out and "Make a Difference in the

Kingdom of God."